Microwave Magic
Cooking for Health

Grolier Limited
TORONTO

Contributors to this series:

Recipes and Technical Assistance:
École de cuisine Bachand-Bissonnette
Cooking consultants:
Denis Bissonette
Michèle Émond
Dietician:
Christiane Barbeau
Photos:
Laramée Morel Communications
Audio-Visuelles
Design:
Claudette Taillefer
Assistants:
Julie Deslauriers
Philippe O'Connor
Joan Pothier
Accessories:
Andrée Cournoyer
Writing:
Communications La Griffe Inc.
Text Consultants:
Cap et bc inc.
Advisors:
Roger Aubin
Joseph R. De Varennes
Gaston Lavoie
Kenneth H. Pearson

Assembly:
Carole Garon
Vital Lapalme
Jean-Pierre Larose
Carl Simmons
Gus Soriano
Marc Vallières
Production Managers:
Gilles Chamberland
Ernest Homewood
Production Assistants:
Martine Gingras
Catherine Gordon
Kathy Kishimoto
Peter Thomlison
Art Director:
Bernard Lamy
Editors:
Laurielle Ilacqua
Susan Marshall
Margaret Oliver
Robin Rivers
Lois Rock
Jocelyn Smyth
Donna Thomson
Dolores Williams
Development:
Le Groupe Polygone Éditeurs Inc.

We wish to thank the following firms, PIER I IMPORTS and LE CACHE POT, for their contribution to the illustration of this set.

The series editors have taken every care to ensure that the information given is accurate. However, no cookbook can guarantee the user successful results. The editors cannot accept any responsibility for the results obtained by following the recipes and recommendations given.

Canadian Cataloguing in Publication Data

Main entry under title:

Cooking for Health

(Microwave magic ; 19)
Translation of: La Cuisine santé.
Includes index.
ISBN 0-7172-2440-6

1. Cookery (Natural foods).   2. Microwave cookery.
I. Series: Microwave magic (Toronto, Ont.) ; 19.

TX832.C874 1988   641.5'637   C88-094218-5

Contents

Microwave Magic is a multi-volume set, with each volume devoted to a particular type of cooking. So, if you are looking for a chicken recipe, you simply go to one of the two volumes that deal with poultry. Each volume has its own index, and the final volume contains a general index to the complete set.

Microwave Magic puts over twelve hundred recipes at your fingertips. You will find it as useful as the microwave oven itself. Enjoy!

Note from the Editor

How to Use this Book

The books in this set have been designed to make your job as easy as possible. As a result, most of the recipes are set out in a standard way.

We suggest that you begin by consulting the information chart for the recipe you have chosen. You will find there all the information you need to decide if you are able to make it: preparation time, cost per serving, level of difficulty, number of calories per serving and other relevant details. Thus, if you have only 30 minutes in which to prepare the evening meal, you will quickly be able to tell which recipe is possible and suits your schedule.

The list of ingredients is always clearly separated from the main text. When space allows, the ingredients are shown together in a photograph so that you can make sure you have them all without rereading the list—

another way of saving your valuable time. In addition, for the more complex recipes we have supplied photographs of the key stages involved either in preparation or serving.

All the dishes in this book have been cooked in a 700 watt microwave oven. If your oven has a different wattage, consult the conversion chart that appears on the following page for cooking times in different types of oven. We would like to emphasize that the cooking times given in the book are a minimum. If a dish does not seem to be cooked enough, you may return it to the oven for a few more minutes. Also, the cooking time can vary according to your ingredients: their water and fat content, thickness, shape and even where they come from. We have therefore left a blank space on each recipe page in which you can note

the cooking time that suits you best. This will enable you to add a personal touch to the recipes that we suggest and to reproduce your best results every time.

Although we have put all the technical information together at the front of this book, we have inserted a number of boxed entries called **MICROTIPS** throughout to explain particular techniques. They are brief and simple, and will help you obtain successful results in your cooking.

With the very first recipe you try, you will discover just how simple microwave cooking can be and how often it depends on techniques you already use for cooking with a conventional oven. If cooking is a pleasure for you, as it is for us, it will be all the more so with a microwave oven. Now let's get on with the food.

The Editor

Key to the Symbols

For ease of reference, the following symbols have been used on the recipe information charts.

The pencil symbol ✏️ is a reminder to write your cooking time in the space provided.

Level of Difficulty

🍴 Easy

🍴🍴 Moderate

🍴🍴🍴 Complex

Cost per Serving

$ Inexpensive

$ $ Moderate

$ $ $ Expensive

Power Levels

All the recipes in this book have been tested in a 700 watt oven. As there are many microwave ovens on the market with different power levels, and as the names of these levels vary from one manufacturer to another, we have decided to give power levels as a percentage. To adapt the power levels given here, consult the chart opposite and the instruction manual for your oven.

Generally speaking, if you have a 500 watt or 600 watt oven you should increase cooking times by about 30% over those given, depending on the actual length of time required. The shorter the original cooking time, the greater the percentage by which it must be lengthened. The 30% figure is only an average. Consult the chart for detailed information on this topic.

Power Levels

HIGH: 100% - 90%	Vegetables (except boiled potatoes and carrots) Soup Sauce Fruits Browning ground beef Browning dish Popcorn
MEDIUM HIGH: 80% - 70%	Rapid defrosting of precooked dishes Muffins Some cakes Hot dogs
MEDIUM: 60% - 50%	Cooking tender meat Cakes Fish Seafood Eggs Reheating Boiled potatoes and carrots
MEDIUM LOW: 40%	Cooking less tender meat Simmering Melting chocolate
DEFROST: 30% **LOW: 30% - 20%**	Defrosting Simmering Cooking less tender meat
WARM: 10%	Keeping food warm Allowing yeast dough to rise

Cooking Time Conversion Chart

700 watts	600 watts*
5 s	11 s
15 s	20 s
30 s	40 s
45 s	1 min
1 min	1 min 20 s
2 min	2 min 40 s
3 min	4 min
4 min	5 min 20 s
5 min	6 min 40 s
6 min	8 min
7 min	9 min 20 s
8 min	10 min 40 s
9 min	12 min
10 min	13 min 30 s
20 min	26 min 40 s
30 min	40 min
40 min	53 min 40 s
50 min	66 min 40 s
1 h	1 h 20 min

* There is very little difference in cooking times between 500 watt ovens and 600 watt ovens.

Eat Your Way to Health

Eating is a wonderful sensory experience. As we sit down at the table, our senses come alive—attractive, colorful food has visual appeal and is itself appetizing. Its aroma stimulates our sense of smell and, as we eat, our senses of touch and taste are awakened, our palates reacting to both the texture of the food and its subtle and exciting flavors.

This enjoyment lasts well beyond mealtime; good food leaves us with a happy and contented feeling. In winter, hot food is particularly comforting.

For all these reasons, food has acquired a value symbolic of something beyond its role as mere fuel. By inviting others to dine, we are offering not only a meal but, above all, hospitality. The sharing of food creates a sense of harmony, which may account for the fact that throughout the world many important decisions and agreements are made over the dinner table.

The saying "You are what you eat" contains a great deal of truth. Our dietary habits—along with many other issues relating to lifestyle—have been questioned in recent years and new ideas and opinions on the proper way to eat have emerged.

In grandmother's day, the type of cookbook that might have been given as a wedding present would have included recipes for a range of heavy, stodgy foods such as pork stews, meat pies and cakes smothered in butter cream. But times have changed. Today, many young people purchase a yoghurt maker or a microwave cookbook on healthy eating when they move to an apartment on their own. Even senior citizens have changed their eating habits; it would not be in the least unusual to see a grandmother happily munching her way through an alfalfa sandwich!

The reason for this change in attitude is obvious. We all know that we tend to eat foods containing too much fat, too much salt, too much sugar and too many chemical additives. We have fallen into the habit of ignoring natural, unrefined foods such as dry legumes, whole wheat bread and brown rice in favor of highly refined foods that provide many empty calories but few real nutrients.

We do, however, have a good excuse. The pressure to eat the wrong kinds of food is enormous. The urban lifestyle forces many people to eat out, be it in fast-food joints or classy restaurants, where the food served leaves a great deal to be desired in terms of nutritional value. Since so many people are caught up in the fast pace of modern life, the food industry caters to their lifestyles by providing convenience foods, which contain a number of preservatives and artificial colors. Such foods have lost much of their nutritional value as a result of processing.

Consuming too much highly refined food is not good for anyone's health. Fortunately, many people have realized the unhealthy consequences of poor eating habits and have made radical changes in their diets. The result? More and more peole are aware of what constitutes a healthy, balanced diet. In addition, they are coming to recognize other important elements of a healthy lifestyle, such as regular exercise and adequate sleep. All these factors contribute to a better quality of life and to a long and happy existence.

Live to Eat or Eat to Live?

Do we eat for pleasure or out of necessity? There is really no answer to this question; eating is both a pleasure and a necessity. Smooth, unblemished skin, a well-proportioned body, good teeth, abundant energy and a calm, cheerful outlook on life are all indicators of radiant good health. Less obvious but also important indicators are strong bones, a healthy appetite and good digestion.

Good health depends on a balanced daily diet. Working out a proper diet requires a certain amount of thought because the way in which foods are digested and absorbed by the body are very complex. Scientists still have much to learn about the link between diet and health, but they are certain about some very basic principles. In general terms, food has four main functions:

- many foods, such as those containing fats and carbohydrates, provide energy for all mental and physical activity;
- other foods, such as those high in protein, are needed to manufacture and to repair body tissue;
- those containing minerals are important in the formation of the bones, teeth, muscles, nerves and blood;
- and finally, vitamins are essential to keep the body in good working order.

Several other factors should be mentioned in connection with this description of a healthy diet. First, the proper amount of each type of nutrient listed above must be eaten. The amount of food required by different people is directly linked to their level of activity. Over a period of time, too little food or not enough of the right type of food can lead to serious deficiencies. On the other hand, overeating leads to obesity and associated health risks. A key point to remember is that healthy eating is based on one main principle—a balanced diet.

A Balanced Diet

A balanced diet means consuming the required quantity of food from each of the four main food groups: milk and dairy products; meat, fish, poultry and alternates; bread and cereals; and fruits and vegetables. These four groups combine to provide the essential nutrients for growth and good health. (Further details concerning each food group are given on pages 13 through 16.)

The body is like a super-computer; it is able to process the nutrients it receives selectively, taking what it needs and eliminating or storing the rest.

Individual needs vary with age, sex and activity level. For example, a growing teenage boy will need types and quantities of food different from those required by a middle-aged woman with a sedentary lifestyle and, similarly, a pregnant woman requires a diet different from that of an elderly man.

To give an example of the variation in individual food requirements we have included the following chart, which compares the nutritional needs of young children with those of adolescents.

Daily Nutritional Requirements of Children and Adolescents

Food Group	Number of Servings*	
	Preschool Children	Adolescents, Age 15 Years
Milk and dairy products	2-1/4 servings	4 servings
Bread and cereals	3 servings	5 servings
Fruits	2 servings	2 servings
Vegetables	2 servings	2 servings
Meat, fish, poultry and alternates	2 servings	2 servings

* See page 17, "Serving Equivalents," for examples of what constitutes one serving.

A Healthy Diet

A healthy diet can be simplicity itself. The secret is to include a significant proportion of whole grains, fruits and vegetables and to ensure that at least 65% of calories consumed come from non-fat sources. A healthy diet should also be low in alcohol, salt and refined sugar.

Also, the number of calories consumed in a day should not, as a general rule, exceed your caloric output. You can avoid putting on weight either by reducing your calorie intake or increasing your level of activity. However, when you cut down on quantity you should not cut down on nutrients such as vitamins and minerals. In other words, if you plan to eat less you will do better to pass on that wedge of sugar pie for dessert rather than on the jacket-baked potato at lunch or on your morning orange juice.

It must be remembered that the nutritional requirements of a woman who is an expectant or nursing mother are much higher than those for the same woman at other times. See the above chart for a comparison between the two.

Daily Nutritional Requirements of Women

Food Group	Number of Servings*	
	Women, Age 30	Pregnant Women, Age 30
Milk and dairy products	2 servings	4 servings
Bread and cereals	4 servings	5 servings
Fruits	2 servings	2 servings
Vegetables	3 servings	3 servings
Meat, fish, poultry and alternates	2 servings	2 servings

* See page 17, "Serving Equivalents," for examples of what constitutes one serving.

MICROTIPS

Three Principles of a Healthy Diet

There are three principles that should be kept in mind by everyone wishing to maintain healthy eating habits.

1. Eat a variety of foods. For example, different vegetables contain different vitamins and minerals. If you keep your diet varied you are more likely to balance your vitamin and mineral intake without the complicated fuss of detailed calculations.

2. Limit your intake of fats, alcohol and salt. A bowl of blueberries topped with fresh cream may taste wonderful but, if you choose to eat cream too often, your cholesterol count may affect your circulation— and your figure won't hesitate to show it!

3. Learn to balance the calories you eat with the calories you burn off. For example, if your occupation involves outdoor physical labor you can allow yourself generous servings at mealtimes. However, if your work keeps you at a desk in an office and you spend your free time at the movics, you must count your calories quite carefully.

The Canadian Food Guide

The Canadian Food Guide is published by the Government of Canada and it provides a basic outline of the requirements for a healthy, balanced diet. It gives flexible guidelines to enable you to choose the right diet for your nutritional and energy requirements. The guide classifies the foods required in a balanced diet into four main groups: milk and dairy products; meat, fish, poultry and alternates; bread and cereals; and fruits and vegetables.

Milk and Dairy Products

Milk plays a primary role in our diets from the time we are born. Milk and dairy products are important sources of calcium and riboflavin. Also, the milk sold in this country is enriched with Vitamin D, a vitamin that facilitates calcium absorption and, therefore, the development of strong bones. Because Vitamin D is scarce in most other foods, milk is the main anti-rickets agent for young, growing children.

Dairy products remain an important part of our diets throughout life. The range of dairy products available today is very varied. There is milk

itself, which can be obtained whole, partly skimmed and skimmed. It is sold fresh, powdered, ultra-heat treated (U.H.T.) or evaporated. Milk is also used to make other delicious products such as yoghurt, buttermilk and cheese. A 45 g (1.5 oz) serving of cheese, for example, can be substituted for 250 mL (1 cup) milk. When you think about the large variety of cheeses on the market today, it becomes obvious that your required daily intake of milk and dairy products should not be a problem. In addition, there

are cream soups, milk-based desserts (such as flans, rice or tapioca puddings and blancmanges), cream itself and ice cream.

Milk is a fragile food and care must be taken in the way in which it is stored. The riboflavin content, an essential growth-promoting member of the Vitamin B complex, is very sensitive to and easily destroyed by light. So, if you buy milk in plastic bags, always check the date on the label so that you know how long it will keep.

Meat, Fish, Poultry and Alternates

Lean meat (such as veal and some cuts of beef), fatty meat (such as lamb and pork products), fish, poultry and eggs are our principle sources of complete proteins. Some other types of food provide an alternate source of protein.

One type is known as legumes and they include navy beans, soybeans, peas, split peas and lentils, which are all vegetables. Nuts provide an alternate source of protein as well. Vegetable proteins are not complete proteins because they do not contain all the essential amino acids, but complete proteins can be obtained by combining some of these vegetable proteins with other types of vegetable protein or with animal protein.

Bread and Cereals

Cereals (such as wheat, corn, millet, rye, barley and oats), root vegetables (such as potatoes) and foods made from these ingredients (such as bread and pasta) are all classed as cereals and form another major food group. Breakfast cereals—particularly oatmeal porridge and corn flakes—are very familiar to us. However, other cereals can play an equally useful part in a balanced diet. Millet and buckwheat are lesser known cereals, but they contain a variety of amino acids and can be combined with foods containing complementary amino acids to yield complete proteins. For example, a slice of six-grain bread (a cereal) spread with peanut butter (a nut) combines to make a food that is rich in protein.

Fruits and Vegetables

Fruits and vegetables provide Vitamin A, Vitamin C, thiamin, folic acid, trace elements and iron. They are also high in fiber. In particular, the leafy vegetables such as spinach, romaine lettuce, escarole, chard, endive, parsley and cress are exceptionally rich in Vitamin A, folic acid and iron. An added bonus is that fruits and vegetables are bright and colorful and, used in their own right or as garnishes, they contribute flare to the presentation of your food.

The Canadian Food Guide: Recommended Daily Intake (in Servings*)

Milk and Dairy Products Children up to age 11: 2 to 3 servings Adolescents and expectant or nursing mothers: 3 to 4 servings Adults: 2 servings	**Bread and Cereals** 3 to 5 servings (It is preferable to choose grain products)
Meat, Fish, Poultry and and Alternates 2 servings, including eggs and cheese at least three times a week and liver occasionally	**Fruits and Vegetables** 4 to 5 servings, of which two should be vegetables

* See page 17, ''Serving Equivalents,'' for examples of what constitutes one serving.

The Nutritional Value of Different Foods

Fats

Lipids, or fatty substances, are essential for our bodies to function properly. However, we do not need large amounts. In fact, we need so little that most of us eat more fat than is necessary. One sad consequence of this tendency is that in North America cardiovascular disorders cause more deaths than any other diseases, including all forms of cancer. One area in which caution must be observed involves our intake of certain foods containing what we refer to as "hidden" fat. Everyone knows that butter, margarine, vegetable oil, salad dressing and mayonnaise contain fatty substances. But it is easy to overlook the fact that they are also found in meat, milk products (with the exception of skim milk products), baked goods, chocolate, cream sauces, nuts and so on. Even people who watch their diets very carefully probably consume more fat than they think.

Serving Equivalents

Fat—1 serving	5 mL (1 teaspoon) butter
	15 mL (1 tablespoon) sauce
	5 mL (/ teaspoon) mayonnaise
Milk and dairy products—1 serving	250 mL (1 cup) milk
	30 g (1 oz) cheese
	175 g (6 oz) yoghurt
Meat—1 serving	30 g (1 oz) cheese
	50 g (1/4 cup) dry legumes
	1 egg
Fruit—1 serving	1 orange
	125 mL (1/2 cup) juice
Vegetables—1 serving	50 mL (1/4 cup) carrots
	125 mL (1/2 cup) green beans
	30 mL (2 tablespoons) corn
Bread and cereals—1 serving	1 slice of bread
	125 mL (1/2 cup) pasta
	125 mL (1/2 cup) rice

Protein

Living organisms cannot exist without protein because their cells are, in effect, made of protein. Essential for growth and strength, protein is particularly important for the development of the muscles, the health of the liver and the production of antibodies. It stimulates the appetite and provides a non-fattening way to satisfy our need for food.

All types of protein consist of chains of amino acids, each amino acid having its place in the chain and performing a specific function. A protein is not complete unless it has the eight essential amino acids. The word "essential" in the description of the amino acids is perfectly justified because food containing incomplete protein cannot be properly used by the body. Most animal sources of protein contain the eight essential amino acids, so meat, poultry, fish and eggs contain complete protein. The same cannot be said of all sources of protein. To obtain complete protein from other sources, you would have to combine vegetable proteins such as legumes (lentils, dried peas, dried beans), cereals, nuts or seeds (peanut butter, sunflower seeds) with animal protein or foods containing complementary proteins. Macaroni and cheese or corn flakes and milk, for example, are combinations that yield complete proteins.

You can also obtain complete proteins from pork and beans served with whole wheat bread or a casserole of rice and lentils. For the amount of protein found in some of the common foods belonging to the food groups outlined in the Canadian Food Guide, consult the charts on pages 20 and 21.

Energy Requirements for Different Activities

Activity	Energy Requirements per Hour (in calories)
Horseback riding (walking)	150
Slow walking	200
Golf	300
Brisk walking	350
Cycling	450
Tennis	450
Horseback riding (trotting)	500
Swimming	700
Running	800-1000

MICROTIPS

Lentils

Of all the legumes, lentils are the most digestible because their cellulose is relatively soft. They are rich in iron, phosphorus, potassium and calcium. You can buy them precooked in cans or you can buy dried lentils and cook them yourself. To prepare dried lentils, you must first soak them in water for 3 to 4 hours, but no longer or they may begin to ferment. Then chop an onion, sauté it lightly in oil, add the lentils and allow them to absorb the oil. Add 500 mL (2 cups) of water for each 250 mL (1 cup) of lentils and cook for about 1-1/2 hours. Add salt at the end of the cooking time. The cooked lentils may then be added to meat dishes (perhaps shepherd's pie) or tomato soup or they may be used as a basis for cream soups.

Delicious!

Carbohydrates

The term "carbohydrates" refers to starches and sugars. Major sources of carbohydrates include potatoes, flour and sugar. They are essential to keep the body functioning but they have the reputation of being fattening. It is true that they will contribute to obesity if eaten in excess because, along with fat, they are a major source of food energy. The important point is not to consume more food energy than you use up in activity (see the chart opposite, on page 18).

Eaten in moderation, carbohydrates are a valuable food. But the distinction between poor quality carbohydrates and good quality carbohydrates should be made clear. The refined sugar sprinkled on your breakfast grapefuit and in the doughnut you eat during your coffee break, or even hidden in alcohol, belongs in the former category. Good quality carbohydrates, on the other hand, provide not merely calories but also vitamins and other nutrients; a cup of brown rice, for example, contains not only carbohydrates but also proteins, minerals and fiber. Quite a bonus to go along with the calories!

If you find you really cannot do without sugar, don't think you are doing yourself a favor by using honey, brown sugar or molasses in its place; these substitutes for sugar contain exactly the same type of sugar as the refined product!

Vitamins

The word "vitamin" was coined when a cure for beriberi was discovered. In one particular village in which this disease was rampant, those investigating it came to realize that the inhabitants lived exclusively on polished rice and concluded that the villagers were suffering from a lack of nutrients found in unprocessed rice. One important nutrient (which we now know as Vitamin B) was called an "amine." This scientific term was joined to the Latin *vita,* meaning life, to produce the word "vitamin"—a substance essential to life.

Today, vitamins are the focus of a great deal of attention. Are they really miracle substances? The proprietors of the pill industry, in selling megadoses of multi-vitamins, would like us to think so. But although the importance of vitamins cannot be dismissed, it is doubtful that anyone who eats a normal, balanced diet suffers any deficiencies. The small quantities of vitamins required by us are present in a wide range of foods. That our vitamin needs are minimal is illustrated by the fact that vitamins are measured not in grams as other nutrients are but in thousandths of grams (milligrams) and international units (I.U.).

Calories and Kilojoules

The calorie is the unit used to measure energy.

Food calories therefore indicate the value of foods as fuel for our physical activities but there is no link between calories and nutritional value. For example, a chocolate bar has very little nutritional value but has many calories (250) whereas a large bowl (250 mL or 1 cup) of fresh strawberries contains only 55 calories—along with 88 mg of Vitamin C and 250 mg of potassium. Which would you choose?

Not everyone has the same requirements for food calories per day. A man who is two meters (six feet) tall needs more food energy for daily activities than an eight-year-old girl. People who take in more calories than required for their daily activities gain weight and those who consume fewer calories than they use in their daily activity lose weight.

There is a very simple way to work out the number of calories you need to maintain your ideal weight. You simply multiply your ideal weight (in pounds) by the number of calories applicable to your age and sex given in the chart on page 20. The answer you obtain represents the number of calories you require daily. If you want to lose or gain weight, adjust the number of calories you consume accordingly.

However, assuming you are at your ideal weight, the following figures constitute general guidelines as to the number of calories rquired to maintain it:
- men: at least 1600 calories per day;
- women: at least 1200 calories per day;
- adolescents: at least 1400 calories per day.

The term "calorie" is one that is being replaced by its metric equivalent—the kilojoule— simply because it is more compatible with other metric measurements currently coming into use (meter, kilogram, and so on). One calorie equals 4.185 kilojoules.

For the number of calories contained in some of the common foods in the four food groups outlined in the Canadian Food Guide, consult the charts on this page and on page 21, opposite.

Microwave Cooking: Retaining the Nutritional Value of Foods

Unlike conventional methods of cooking, microwave cooking retains the nutritional value of foods as well as their taste, texture and color. This aspect of microwave cooking is particularly true for fruits and vegetables.

Microwave cooking requires very little water because it makes use of the water already present in the food being cooked. In fact, foods that have a high water content need no water for cooking and therefore can be cooked without losing any of the

Calculating Basal Metabolism

Age	Women	Men
45 years or less	10 calories	11 calories
Over 45 years	9 calories	10 calories

The Nutritional Value of Some Common Foods

Milk and Dairy Products

Food	Quantity	Calories	Protein (g)	Calcium (mg)	Vit. A (I.U.)
Cheddar cheese	30 g (1 oz)	114	7	204	360
Frozen milk desserts	125 mL (1/2 cup)	143	4	186	280
Ice cream	125 mL (1/2 cup)	123	3	133	410
Skim milk	250 mL (1 cup)	90	9	320	528
Whole milk	250 mL (1 cup)	160	8	308	325
2% milk	250 mL (1 cup)	123	8	314	528
Yoghurt	150 mL (2/3 cup)	115	8	221	130

Bread and Cereals

Food	Quantity	Calories	Protein g	Calcium mg
Bread, whole wheat	1 slice	70	3	30
Pasta (enriched)	250 mL (1 cup) cooked	164	5	20
Porridge oats	250 mL (1 cup) cooked	218	7.6	42
Rice, brown	250 mL (1 cup) cooked	232	4.9	30

water-soluble vitamins they contain. Similarly, the natural vitamins that are sensitive to heat are less likely to be completely destroyed because microwaving reduces the cooking time for nearly all foods.

We offer the following tips on microwave cooking to enable you to cut down your cooking time, thereby retaining the maximum nutritional value in the food being prepared.

The size and density of the food being cooked and the temperature used affect the cooking time; a chicken thigh will obviously cook more quickly than a large roast of beef.

When you cook foods together, cut them so that they are all roughly the same size.

Frozen foods will need to cook longer than refrigerated foods or those that are at room temperature.

To minimize water loss, cover foods when you cook them. This precaution will further reduce the need for extra water.

Food in the center of a dish will cook more slowly than that around the edge. As a result, you should stir the food or give the dish a half-turn during the cooking time. It is also important to remember that cooking continues for a short period after the food is taken out of the oven. As a result, you should remove the food just before it is fully cooked and allow a brief standing period before you serve it.

Fruits and Vegetables

Food	Quantity	Calories	Vit. C (mg)	Calcium (mg)	Vit. A (I.U.)
Apple	1	70	3	8	50
Banana	1	85	10	8	230
Cantaloupe	1/2	60	63	38	9200
Orange	1	60	240	49	260
Orange juice	125 mL (1/2 cup)	54	61	13	250
Pear	1	100	7	13	30
Broccoli, cooked	125 mL (1/2 cup)	23	74	70	1940
Cabbage, cooked	250 mL (1 cup)	30	2	64	190
Green pepper, cooked or raw	1	15	1	7	310

Meat, Fish, Poultry and Alternates

Food	Quantity	Calories	Protein (g)
Chicken breast	90 g (3 oz)	149	28.2
Fillet of sole	90 g (3 oz)	85	18
Macaroni and cheese	250 mL (1 cup)	470	28
Pork and beans 250 mL (1 cup) milk	250 mL (1 cup)	287	19
Steak, lean and fat (broiled)	90 g (3 oz)	330	20

Soups

Dinner's ready! A large tureen is carried into the dining room and placed on the table. Off comes the lid. Mmm! What a delicious aroma. The soup is ladled into bowls and there is plenty for everyone. It brings back memories of old-fashioned family get-togethers.

But soup is still an everyday favorite. Our busy lifestyles mean that we sometimes must forget about homemade soup, lovingly simmered throughout the day to create a perfect blend of flavors, and opt instead for one out of a package or a can. With a microwave oven, however, you can put a soup together in minutes, cook it in less than 30—and relax a little before the meal.

Probably the most popular type of soup is that made with a good stock as its base and a variety of other ingredients that are usually diced or puréed. These ingredients frequently include meat, vegetables, pasta, rice or, sometimes, even bread.

A different type of soup, made from a slice of bread soaked in milk or stock, was very common at one time. This combination was known in English as a sop but, in Anglo-Saxon cooking traditions, it diminished in popularity. The same technique, however, can be found today in the French tradition, the most popular example being French onion soup. A much thinner type of soup than most, it relies on the bread to make it a substantial meal. It is interesting to see the way in which fashions change—to the extent that many people now think that somehow it is not proper to dip bread in soup!

Over the centuries, different soups have developed into classics. Minestrone, an Italian soup made from vegetables and rice, is one. Another is bouillabaisse, a Provençale speciality made from a variety of fish. There are thousands of other soups, and it would be hopeless to try to list them all. There is consommé, made from reduced meat stock, bisque, made from seafood broth, and the celebrated turtle soup. Most soups are served hot but some, such as the Spanish tomato soup known as gazpacho and the classic leek and potato vichyssoise, are served cold.

Whatever the soup—whether it be thick or thin, cream or broth, bisque or chowder, regional or national, hot or cold—there are two important points to be kept in mind. First, soups are one of the most versatile foods on any menu; they can be served as appetizers for formal full-course meals or as meals in their own right, for lunches or light, informal suppers. And second, the ingredients used to make them are normally full of nutrients, giving soups the happy reputation of being one of the healthiest foods around.

Broad Bean Soup

Level of Difficulty	🍴
Preparation Time	20 min
Cost per Serving	**$**
Number of Servings	12
Nutritional Value	98 calories 3.8 g protein 1.2 mg iron
Food Exchanges	1 oz meat 1 vegetable exchange
Cooking Time	58 min
Standing Time	5 min
Power Level	100%
Write Your Cooking Time Here	✏️🍎

Ingredients
500 mL (2 cups) broad beans
30 g (1 oz) salt bacon, chopped
250 mL (1 cup) carrots, diced
250 mL (1 cup) celery, chopped
1 onion, chopped
1.75 L (7 cups) water
30 mL (2 tablespoons) fine herbs
125 mL (1/2 cup) barley
salt and pepper to taste

Method
— Shell the broad beans and set aside.
— Put the bacon in a deep dish and cook at 100% for 1 minute.
— Stir in the carrots, celery, onion and broad beans and add 50 mL (1/4 cup) of the water.
— Cover and cook at 100% for 10 to 12 minutes, or until the vegetables are done but still firm. Stir once during the cooking time.
— Add the remaining water and all the ingredients.
— Cover and continue to cook at 100% for 35 to 45 minutes, stirring twice.
— Allow to stand for 5 minutes before serving.

This traditional soup is always popular and has the added advantages of being economical and easy to make. This picture shows the ingredients you should assemble before you begin to cook.

Shell the broad beans and set them aside.

Cook the vegetables with the bacon and 50 mL (1/4 cup) of the water. Cover and cook at 100% for 10 to 12 minutes, stirring once during the cooking time.

Pumpkin Soup

Level of Difficulty	 (icon)
Preparation Time	30 min
Cost per Serving	$
Number of Servings	8
Nutritional Value	53 calories 10 g carbohydrate 37.2 mg calcium
Food Exchanges	2 vegetable exchanges
Cooking Time	38 min
Standing Time	None
Power Level	100%
Write Your Cooking Time Here	

Ingredients
500 mL (2 cups) pumpkin, diced
500 mL (2 cups) potatoes, diced
125 mL (1/2 cup) celery, diced
125 mL (1/2 cup) carrots, diced
2 leeks, diced
1 clove garlic, crushed
1 L (4 cups) chicken stock
2 mL (1/2 teaspoon) thyme
1 bay leaf
salt and pepper to taste
125 mL (1/2 cup) 2% milk

Method
— Put the potatoes, celery, carrots, leeks and garlic into a deep dish and add 125 mL (1/2 cup) of the chicken stock.
— Cover and cook at 100% for 6 to 8 minutes, stirring once.
— Add the remaining stock and the other ingredients (except the milk).
— Cover and continue to cook at 100% for 15 to 25 minutes, stirring once.
— Remove the bay leaf and purée the soup in a blender.
— Heat at 100% for 3 to 5 minutes.
— Stir in the milk just before serving.

Fisherman's Soup

Level of Difficulty	⚔️
Preparation Time	25 min
Cost per Serving	$ $
Number of Servings	8
Nutritional Value	134 calories 11 g protein 9.3 g carbohydrate
Food Exchanges	2 oz meat 1 vegetable exchange 1/4 milk exchange
Cooking Time	25 min
Standing Time	None
Power Level	100%
Write Your Cooking Time Here	

Ingredients
500 mL (2 cups) salmon, cooked
125 mL (1/2 cup) shrimp, cooked
250 mL (1 cup) potatoes, cubed
1 onion, chopped
125 mL (1/2 cup) celery, cubed
250 mL (1 cup) tomatoes, peeled and chopped
300 mL (1-1/4 cups) boiling water
2 mL (1/2 teaspoon) celery seed
2 mL (1/2 teaspoon) thyme
15 mL (1 tablespoon) parsley, chopped
salt and pepper to taste
30 mL (2 tablespoons) butter
30 mL (2 tablespoons) flour
500 mL (2 cups) 2% milk

Method
— Put the vegetables into a large bowl and then add the boiling water and the seasonings.
— Cover and cook at 100% for 10 to 12 minutes, stirring once during the cooking time.
— Add the salmon and shrimp; cover and set aside.
— Melt the butter at 100% for 30 seconds.
— Add the flour and mix well.
— Whisk in the milk and cook at 100% for 6 to 8 minutes, stirring twice during the cooking time.
— Add the thickened milk to the salmon, shrimp and vegetables, stirring carefully.
— Heat at 100% for 3 to 5 minutes, stirring once during the cooking time.

Assemble all the ingredients for this delicious recipe before you begin to cook.

Cook the vegetables with the water and seasonings in a covered dish.

Carefully add the milk mixture to the salmon, shrimp and vegetables, stirring constantly.

Broccoli and Onion Soup

Level of Difficulty	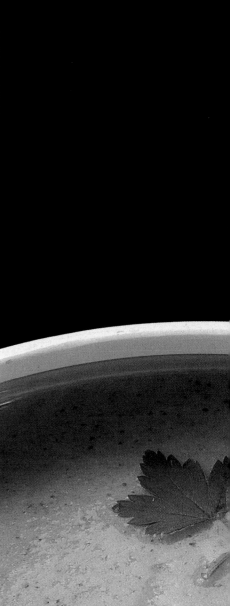
Preparation Time	20 min
Cost per Serving	**$**
Number of Servings	4
Nutritional Value	110 calories 10.5 g carbohydrate 81.3 mg Vitamin C
Food Exchanges	2 vegetable exchanges 1-1/4 fat exchanges
Cooking Time	19 min
Standing Time	None
Power Level	100%
Write Your Cooking Time Here	

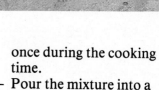

Ingredients
1 small head of broccoli, cut into flowerets
30 mL (2 tablespoons) butter
1 red onion, finely chopped
1 clove garlic, finely chopped
1 potato, diced
750 mL (3 cups) chicken stock
50 mL (1/4 cup) fresh parsley, chopped
salt and pepper to taste

Method
— Put the butter in a dish and add the onion, garlic and potato.
— Cover and cook at 100% for 4 minutes, stirring once during the cooking time.
— Add the broccoli, cover again and continue to cook at 100% for 3 to 4 minutes, stirring once.
— Add the remaining ingredients; cover and continue to cook at 100% for 5 to 6 minutes, stirring once during the cooking time.
— Pour the mixture into a blender and purée at high speed for a few seconds until smooth.
— Check the seasoning and adjust to taste.
— Heat at 100% for 3 to 5 minutes, stirring once during the cooking time.

This soup will set a well-balanced meal off to a good start. Here are the ingredients you should assemble before you begin to cook.

Add the broccoli to the mixture of onion, garlic and potato and continue to cook at 100% for 3 to 4 minutes, stirring once.

Add the chicken stock, parsley, salt and pepper to the vegetables. Cook at 100% for 5 to 6 minutes and then purée the soup in the blender.

Lentil and Tomato Soup

Level of Difficulty	🍴
Preparation Time	10 min
Cost per Serving	**$**
Number of Servings	8
Nutritional Value	77 calories 6.9 g protein 14 g carbohydrate
Food Exchanges	0.5 oz meat 1/2 vegetable exchange 1/2 bread exchange
Cooking Time	19 min
Standing Time	5 min
Power Level	100%
Write Your Cooking Time Here	

Ingredients
225 g (8 oz) lentils, cooked
1 540 mL (19 oz) can tomatoes
1.5 L (6 cups) hot chicken stock
1 onion, diced
1 clove garlic, chopped
1 stick celery, diced
1 bay leaf
salt and pepper to taste

Method
— Pour 125 mL (1/2 cup) of the chicken stock into a deep dish and add the lentils, onion, garlic and celery.
— Cover and cook at 100% for 4 to 5 minutes, stirring once during the cooking time.
— Add the tomatoes, the remaining stock and the bay leaf; season to taste.
— Cover again and cook at 100% for 12 to 14 minutes, stirring once during the cooking time.
— Leave the cover on the dish and allow to stand for 5 minutes.

Celery Soup

Level of Difficulty	🍴
Preparation Time	15 min
Cost per Serving	$
Number of Servings	6
Nutritional Value	43 calories 4.8 g carbohydrate
Food Exchanges	2 vegetable exchanges
Cooking Time	32 min
Standing Time	None
Power Level	100%
Write Your Cooking Time Here	

Ingredients
1 bunch celery with its leaves, thinly sliced
75 mL (1/3 cup) water
15 mL (1 tablespoon) butter
1 onion, chopped
1 clove garlic, chopped
1 pear, peeled and chopped
500 mL (2 cups) chicken stock
500 mL (2 cups) vegetable stock
salt and pepper to taste

Method
— Pour the water into a dish and add the celery.
— Cover and cook at 100% for 8 to 10 minutes, stirring once during the cooking time and set aside.
— In another dish melt the butter and add the onion and the garlic; cook at 100% for 2 minutes.
— Add the chopped pear; cover and continue to cook at 100% for 3 to 4 minutes.
— Stir this mixture into the cooked celery, add both the chicken and the vegetable stock and season to taste.
— Cover and cook at 100% for 10 minutes, stirring once during the cooking time.
— Pour the mixture into a blender and purée for a few seconds until smooth.
— Heat at 100% for 4 to 6 minutes, stirring once during the cooking time.

This combination of ingredients enables you to put together a truly exquisite soup in no time.

MICROTIPS

A Garlic Substitute

If you find that you have run out of garlic, you can use garlic salt instead. However, take care not to add it until the recipe directs you to add the seasonings because the sodium in the salt will cause the ingredients to dry out and possibly burn if it is added before they are put into the microwave oven.

Vichyssoise

Level of Difficulty	🍴
Preparation Time	20 min*
Cost per Serving	$
Number of Servings	6
Nutritional Value	48 calories 7.8 g carbohydrate 48.8 mg calcium
Food Exchanges	1 vegetable exchange
Cooking Time	16 min
Standing Time	None
Power Level	100%
Write Your Cooking Time Here	

* This soup must be chilled before serving.

Ingredients
2 leeks, thinly sliced
1 onion, chopped
1 stick celery, thinly sliced
1 potato, sliced
750 mL (3 cups) hot chicken stock
pinch nutmeg
a few drops Tabasco sauce
175 mL (3/4 cup) 2% milk
salt and pepper to taste
parsley to garnish

Method
— Put all the vegetables into a dish and add 75 mL (1/3 cup) of the chicken stock.
— Cover and cook at 100% for 6 to 8 minutes, stirring once during the cooking time.
— Add the remaining stock, the nutmeg and the Tabasco sauce.
— Cook at 100% for 6 to 8 minutes, stirring once during the cooking time.
— Pour the mixture into a blender and purée for a few seconds until smooth and creamy.
— Stir in the milk and season to taste.
— Chill and garnish with parsley before serving.

This soup will quickly become a summertime favorite. Here are the ingredients that should be assembled before you begin to cook.

Add 75 mL (1/3 cup) of the chicken stock to the vegetables; cover and cook at 100% for 6 to 8 minutes.

Add the remaining stock, nutmeg and Tabasco sauce before the final stage of cooking.

After puréeing the ingredients, stir in the milk and season to taste. Chill the soup before serving.

Starters

Who would argue with the belief that good conversation is as important to the truly enjoyable meal as good food? Starters, whether offered in the form of cocktail hors d'oeuvres or appetizers served at the table, are a great asset to this aspect of entertaining. They give you the opportunity to gather your guests together to relax and chat while enjoying small portions of food and whetting their appetites for the courses to follow.

Starters are the imaginative cook's delight because they can be as fanciful as desired. One traditional approach to serving the appetizer is simply to offer a small serving of vegetables or a modest portion of a main dish; another is to serve a selection of raw vegetables, or crudités, such as carrot sticks, slices of green and red pepper, mushrooms and cauliflower or broccoli flowerets with an accompanying dip. However, in many cases professional chefs and amateur cooks alike will take this opportunity to try out more innovative recipes. A great starter sets the tone for the remainder of the meal and so it is worth some effort.

Choose your starter carefully. It is essential to keep in mind the dishes that are to follow—they should complement each other in terms of flavor, texture and color as well as provide a balance of nutrients. Some combinations are therefore obviously to be avoided. For instance, it would be inappropriate to serve Coquilles Saint-Jacques as an appetizer if you are planning Tuna Florentine as the main dish!

A vegetable starter is usually a safe bet—perhaps Vegetables au Gratin (page 44) or Zucchini and Tomatoes in Scallop Shells (page 50)—to provide an interesting, tasty and nutritious appetizer.

Braised Vegetables

Level of Difficulty	
Preparation Time	30 min
Cost per Serving	$
Number of Servings	6
Nutritional Value	93 calories 18.1 g carbohydrate 34.7 mg Vitamin C
Food Exchanges	2 vegetable exchanges 1 fat exchange
Cooking Time	9 min
Standing Time	3 min
Power Level	100%
Write Your Cooking Time Here	

Ingredients
1 onion, thinly sliced
1 clove garlic, crushed
1 green pepper, cut into strips
1 red pepper, cut into strips
450 g (1 lb) snow peas
225 g (8 oz) bean sprouts
1 carrot, grated
30 mL (2 tablespoons) oil
1 apple, coarsely chopped
30 mL (2 tablespoons) soy sauce
30 mL (2 tablespoons) sherry

Method
— Preheat a browning dish at 100% for 7 minutes, add the oil and heat at 100% for 30 seconds.
— Sauté the onion, garlic, peppers, snow peas, bean sprouts and carrot.
— Cover and cook at 100% for 4 to 6 minutes, or until the vegetables are cooked but still crisp. Stir once during the cooking time.
— Add the apple, soy sauce and sherry.
— Cover again and continue to cook at 100% for 2 to 3 minutes, stirring once during the cooking time.
— Allow to stand for 3 minutes before serving.

This braised vegetable recipe goes very well with most main dishes. Begin by assembling these ingredients.

Preheat the browning dish, add the oil, and sauté the vegetables in the hot oil.

After the first cooking period, add the apple, soy sauce and sherry.

Ratatouille with Chick Peas

Level of Difficulty	
Preparation Time	20 min
Cost per Serving	$
Number of Servings	4
Nutritional Value	180 calories 11.3 g protein 38.6 g carbohydrate
Food Exchanges	1 oz meat 2 vegetable exchanges 1 bread exchange
Cooking Time	25 min
Standing Time	3 min
Power Level	100%
Write Your Cooking Time Here	

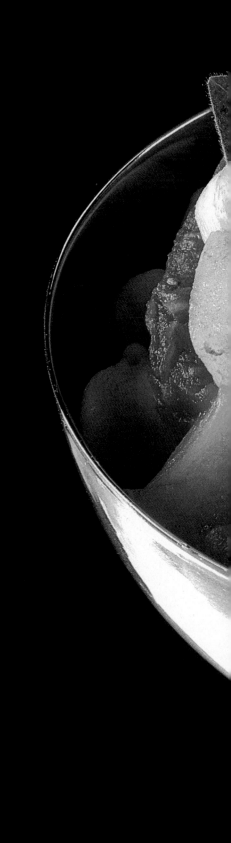

Ingredients
1 540 mL (19 oz) can Italian-style tomatoes
2 red onions, chopped
2 zucchini, thinly sliced
1 eggplant, peeled and diced
2 cloves garlic, chopped
10 mL (2 teaspoons) oregano
salt and pepper to taste
1 540 mL (19 oz) can chick peas, drained

Method
— Drain the tomatoes and reserve the juice.
— Put the onions, zucchini, eggplant and the juice from the tomatoes in a dish; cover and cook at 100% for 6 to 7 minutes, stirring once during the cooking time.
— Add the tomatoes, garlic and oregano and season to taste. Cover again and continue to cook at 100% for 8 to 10 minutes, stirring once during the cooking time.
— Rinse the chick peas and add them to the mixture.
— Cover and cook at 100% for 6 to 8 minutes, stirring once during the cooking time.
— Allow to stand for 3 minutes before serving.

42

Vegetables au Gratin

Level of Difficulty	(utensils icon)
Preparation Time	20 min
Cost per Serving	$
Number of Servings	4
Nutritional Value	137 calories 11.9 g protein 10.7 g carbohydrate
Food Exchanges	1 oz meat 1-1/2 vegetable exchanges 1/4 milk exchange
Cooking Time	14 min
Standing Time	3 min
Power Level	100%, 90%
Write Your Cooking Time Here	

Ingredients
250 mL (1 cup) cauliflower, cut into small flowerets
250 mL (1 cup) broccoli, cut into small flowerets
30 mL (2 tablespoons) water
250 mL (1 cup) mushrooms, thinly sliced
2 slices cooked ham, cut into strips
125 mL (1/2 cup) mozzarella cheese, grated
paprika to garnish

Béchamel Sauce:
30 mL (2 tablespoons) cornstarch
50 mL (1/4 cup) cold water
175 mL (3/4 cup) 2% milk
pinch nutmeg
pinch fine herbs
salt and pepper to taste

Method
— Make the béchamel sauce by mixing together the cornstarch and water and adding the milk.
— Add the nutmeg and the fine herbes and season to taste.
— Cook at 100% for 3 to 4 minutes or until the sauce thickens, stirring twice during the cooking time, and set aside.
— Next, put the cauliflower and broccoli in a dish and add 30 mL (2 tablespoons) water; cover and cook at 100% for 4 to 5 minutes, stirring once during the cooking time.
— Arrange the vegetables in an au gratin dish and place the mushrooms and the ham on top.
— Pour the béchamel sauce over the vegetable

mixture; add the grated mozzarella and garnish with paprika.
— Cook at 90% for 4 to 5 minutes, giving the dish a half-turn halfway through the cooking time.
— Allow to stand for 3 minutes before serving.

MICROTIPS

Knowing When Vegetables Have Lost Their Nutrients

Vegetables are relatively fragile and must be stored carefully, at the supermarket as well as at home, in order to retain as many nutrients as possible. Remember that a damaged, wilted or moldy vegetable has lost much of its food value. Leafy vegetables, for example, have lost nearly all of their Vitamin C once they have wilted. It is therefore important to select carefully when you are buying vegetables— by paying attention, you will soon learn to recognize those that are the freshest.

Rice with Tofu, Oriental Style

Level of Difficulty	🍴
Preparation Time	20 min
Cost per Serving	$
Number of Servings	4
Nutritional Value	268 calories 16.2 g protein 33.3 g carbohydrate
Food Exchanges	2 oz meat 1/2 vegetable exchange 1-1/2 bread exchanges
Cooking Time	28 min
Standing Time	5 min
Power Level	100%, 70%
Write Your Cooking Time Here	

Ingredients
375 mL (1-1/2 cups) long grain rice
750 mL (3 cups) boiling water
5 mL (1 teaspoon) salt
15 mL (1 tablespoon) butter
50 mL (1/4 cup) green onions, thinly sliced
1 clove garlic, thinly sliced
125 mL (1/2 cup) mushrooms, thinly sliced
125 mL (1/2 cup) water, to make the sauce
30 mL (2 tablespoons) ketchup
10 mL (2 teaspoons) soy sauce
2 mL (1/2 teaspoon) crushed red chili peppers
675 g (1-1/2 lb) tofu, diced
10 mL (2 teaspoons) cornstarch
30 mL (2 tablespoons) water

Method
— Pour the boiling water into a dish and add the salt and rice.
— Cover and cook at 100% for 7 minutes.
— Reduce the power to 70% and cook for 10 to 12 minutes, or until the rice is done.
— Leave the cover on the dish and allow to stand for 5 minutes; set aside.
— Put the butter in another dish and add the green onions and garlic; cover and cook at 100% for 1 minute.
— Add the mushrooms and continue to cook at 100% for 2 minutes.
— Stir in 125 mL (1/2 cup) water, the ketchup, soy sauce and the chili peppers.
— Cook at 100% for 2 minutes, stirring once during the cooking time.
— Add the tofu; cover and cook at 100% for 2

minutes, stirring once during the cooking time.
— Dissolve the cornstarch in the water and add to the mixture.
— Cook at 100% for 1 to 2 minutes, or until the mixture thickens.
— Pour the mixture over the rice before serving.

Cover the rice and cook at 100% for 7 minutes. Reduce the power to 70% and cook for 10 to 12 minutes longer.

MICROTIPS

Rice as Fiber

To increase the amount of food fiber in a chicken and rice casserole, use brown rice rather than white, or use a mixture of the two.

Harvard Beets

Level of Difficulty	🍴
Preparation Time	10 min
Cost per Serving	**$**
Number of Servings	3
Nutritional Value	122 calories 19.7 g carbohydrate
Food Exchanges	1 vegetable exchange 5 g carbohydrate 1 fat exchange
Cooking Time	4 min
Standing Time	5 min
Power Level	100%
Write Your Cooking Time Here	

Ingredients
1 398 mL (14 oz) can sliced beets
30 mL (2 tablespoons) brown sugar
15 mL (1 tablespoon) cornstarch
50 mL (1/4 cup) white wine
30 mL (2 tablespoons) lemon juice
2 cloves
salt and pepper to taste
15 mL (1 tablespoon) butter

Method
— Drain the beets and reserve 30 mL (2 tablespoons) of the liquid.
— Combine the brown sugar and cornstarch in a dish.
— Add the wine, lemon juice, beet liquid and cloves and stir well.
— Cook at 100% for 1 to 2 minutes, stirring once during the cooking time.
— Add the beets and cook at 100% for 2 minutes, stirring once during the cooking time, and season to taste.
— Allow to stand for 5 minutes.
— Remove the cloves and add the butter before serving.

48

Beets prepared in this way can be served hot or cold and they will complement a great many main dishes. Here are the ingredients that you should assemble before cooking them.

Cook the sauce ingredients together at 100% for 1 to 2 minutes.

Add the beets to the sauce before the final stage of cooking.

Zucchini and Tomatoes in Scallop Shells

Level of Difficulty	¶¶
Preparation Time	15 min
Cost per Serving	$
Number of Servings	4
Nutritional Value	176 calories 13.9 g protein 12.9 g carbohydrate
Food Exchanges	1.5 oz meat 2 vegetable exchanges
Cooking Time	9 min
Standing Time	3 min
Power Level	100%
Write Your Cooking Time Here	

Ingredients
2 zucchini, thinly sliced
4 tomatoes, thinly sliced
5 mL (1 teaspoon) oil
1 clove garlic, crushed
1 large onion, thinly sliced
5 mL (1 teaspoon) thyme
salt and pepper to taste
250 mL (1 cup) mozzarella
cheese, grated
50 mL (1/4 cup) Parmesan
cheese, grated
paprika to garnish
4 scallop shells

Method
— Mix the oil with the garlic
and brush over the scallop
shells.
— Place the sliced onion in
the shells and cook at
100% for 1-1/2 minutes.
— Add the tomatoes,
zucchini and seasoning.
— Top each shell with the
grated mozzarella.
— Sprinkle with the
Parmesan cheese and
paprika.
— Cover the shells with
plastic wrap and cook at
100% for 6 to 8 minutes,
giving them a half-turn
halfway through the
cooking time.
— Allow to stand for 3
minutes before serving.

⟹

Zucchini and Tomatoes in Scallop Shells

You can have these scallop shells ready in less than 30 minutes once you have assembled all these ingredients.

Brush the scallop shells with the mixture of oil and garlic.

Place a layer of tomatoes and then a layer of zucchini on top of the cooked onion in each shell.

Top each shell with grated mozzarella cheese.

Sprinkle with Parmesan cheese and paprika before the final cooking period.

Give the shells a half-turn halfway through the cooking time to ensure even cooking.

MICROTIPS

Color Your Pasta!

Color provides a fanciful touch to homemade pasta.

Yellow:

A pinch of saffron will give your pasta a splendid yellow color. It should be mixed with the flour before other ingredients are added.

Orange:

Add a little tomato purée or pumpkin that has been cooked and finely chopped or puréed to the ingredients for the pasta dough and mix well.

Speckled Green:

Finely chopped fresh herbs or ground dried herbs create this intriguing effect. You can use Basil, fennel, tarragon, marjoram, sorrel, parsley and thyme can be used, and the quantities can be adjusted to your liking. To color 450 g (1 lb) pasta, use 90 mL (6 tablespoons) herbs.

Veal Ramekins

Ingredients
450 g (1 lb) lean ground veal
250 mL (1 cup) water
15 mL (1 tablespoon) onion, finely chopped

15 mL (1 tablespoon) green pepper, finely chopped
15 mL (1 tablespoon) allspice
5 mL (1 teaspoon) cinnamon
pinch garlic powder

10 mL (2 teaspoons) powdered chicken concentrate
1 package unflavored gelatin
125 mL (1/2 cup) cold water

Method
— Combine all the ingredients except the gelatin and cold water in a large bowl and mix well.
— Cook at 100% for 15 minutes, stirring every 5 minutes.
— Sprinkle the gelatin on top of the cold water and leave to soften for 5 minutes.
— Heat the gelatin and water at 100% for 1 minute or until the gelatin dissolves.
— Add the gelatin to the meat and mix well.
— Dip 6 ramekins in cold water.
— Fill each ramekin with an equal amount of the meat mixture.
— Refrigerate until ready to serve.

Level of Difficulty	🍴
Preparation Time	15 min*
Cost per Serving	$
Number of Servings	6
Nutritional Value	140 calories 18 g protein 0.2 g carbohydrate
Food Exchanges	2 oz meat
Cooking Time	16 min
Standing Time	None
Power Level	100%
Write Your Cooking Time Here	✏️🍎

* The ramekins must be chilled before serving.

Main Dishes

When friends ask what you had for dinner the night before, the chances are that you will name the main course. It is the focus of any meal—the part that we count on to satisfy our appetites.

In most cases the major protein portion of the meal is served as the main course. In Western cooking, this course is traditionally based on meat, poultry or fish, which may be served with vegetables or combined with other ingredients for form a complete meal. The recipes for Mexican Beef Stew (page 66) and Fisherman's Stew (page 80) given in this volume are examples of the latter.

Given the current trend of cooking for health, however, some main dishes now include only a small amount of meat or none at all. Therefore, other foods must assume the principal role, notably, dry legumes—which are the next most important source of protein. Aside from our traditional pork and beans (navy beans in sauce with only traces of meat), there is couscous which is an Eastern dish that uses wheat semolina in a stew made with vegetables and chick peas. Couscous can be served with very little meat or none at all, as desired. Chili, a highly spiced dish with red kidney beans and tomatoes, is Mexican in origin and has become very popular in this country. With its large proportion of kidney beans, it goes without saying that chili, like couscous, can be served with or without meat. Manicotti with Spinach (page 84), an innovative main dish with cottage cheese as its major source of protein, should prove to be a popular recipe. These exotic dishes demonstrate just how delicious and nutritious meatless meals can be. And furthermore, the microwave oven has proved to be an efficient tool in the cooking of them.

Whether you are cooking simple, everyday food or for a special occasion, exotic or traditional food, unpretentious food or food that is quite spectacular, the way in which you prepare your main dishes provides you with the opportunity to show off your cooking skills and to display your nutritional sense.

Chicken Stuffed with Cheese

Level of Difficulty	▯▯
Preparation Time	20 min
Cost per Serving	$
Number of Servings	4
Nutritional Value	398 calories 37.3 g protein 268 mg calcium
Food Exchanges	4 oz meat 2 fat exchanges
Cooking Time	15 min
Standing Time	4 min
Power Level	100%, 70%
Write Your Cooking Time Here	

Ingredients
4 chicken breast halves, each weighing 225 g (8 oz), skinned and boned
115 g (4 oz) cheddar cheese slices
1 egg
30 mL (2 tablespoons) Parmesan cheese, grated
5 mL (1 teaspoon) parsley, chopped
pepper to taste
30 mL (2 tablespoons) flour
45 mL (3 tablespoons) oil

Method
— Using a very sharp knife, cut a slit into the flesh along the thickest side of the chicken breast halves to form a pocket in each.
— Cut the cheese slices in two and place two half slices in each breast pocket; press the edges together to close and set aside.
— Beat the egg and add the Parmesan cheese, parsley and pepper.
— Dredge the chicken breast halves with the flour and dip them into the egg and cheese mixture.
— Preheat a browning dish at 100% for 7 minutes; add the oil and heat at 100% for 30 seconds.
— Sear the chicken breasts.
— Reduce the power level to 70% and cook covered for 12 to 15 minutes; halfway through the cooking time, rearrange the breasts so that those parts facing the center now face outwards.
— Allow to stand for 4 minutes before serving.

This delicious and sophisticated dish is so easy to prepare that you could easily serve it on a week night.

Use a very sharp knife to cut a slit into the flesh along the thickest side of each chicken breast half.

Cut the cheese slices into two and place two pieces in each chicken breast. Set aside.

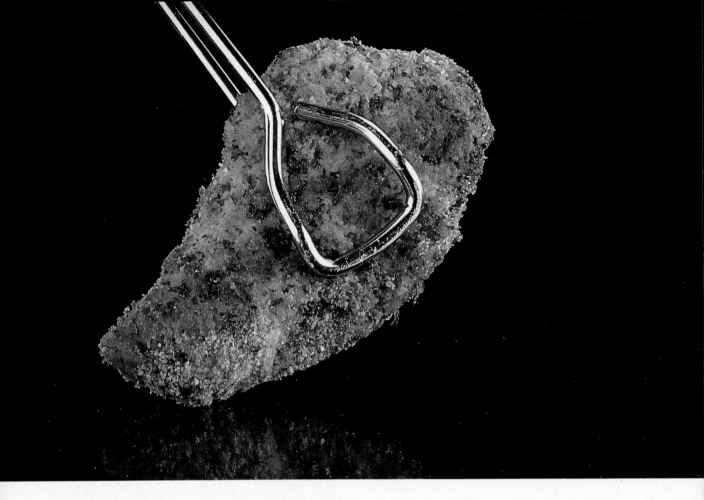

Chicken with Apricots

Level of Difficulty	🍴🍴
Preparation Time	15 min
Cost per Serving	$
Number of Servings	4
Nutritional Value	290 calories 34.8 g protein 4.2 mg iron
Food Exchanges	3 oz meat 1 fruit exchange 1/2 bread exchange
Cooking Time	15 min
Standing Time	3 min
Power Level	100%, 70%
Write Your Cooking Time Here	

Ingredients
4 chicken breast halves, each weighing 175 g (6 oz), skinned and boned
225 g (8 oz) dried apricots
5 mL (1 teaspoon) tarragon
175 mL (3/4 cup) breadcrumbs
60 mL (4 tablespoons) parsley, chopped
1 egg, beaten
30 mL (2 tablespoons) sunflower oil

Method
— Using a very sharp knife, cut a slit into the flesh along the thickest side of each chicken breast half to form a pocket.
— Stuff each pocket with about 60 g (2 oz) apricots and 1 mL (1/4 teaspoon) tarragon.
— Secure the opening with a

toothpick if necessary and set aside.
— Combine the breadcrumbs with the parsley in a bowl.
— Dip the chicken breast halves in the beaten egg and then coat them with the breadcrumbs.
— Preheat a browning dish at 100% for 7 minutes; add the oil and heat at 100% for 30 seconds.
— Sear the chicken breasts.
— Reduce the power level to 70% and cook for 7 minutes.
— Turn the chicken breasts over, rearranging them so that those parts facing the center now face outwards.
— Continue to cook at 70% for 6 to 8 minutes.
— Allow to stand for 3 minutes before serving.

MICROTIPS

To Dry Fresh Herbs

To increase the time that large quantities of parsley, tarragon or any other fresh herb can be safely stored, dry them in the microwave oven.

Place the herbs between two sheets of paper towel and cook them at 100% for 30 seconds to 1 minute, or until you can crumble them with your fingers. Be careful when you use this method, however, because herbs that are left too long in the microwave could burst into flames.

Chicken with Apricots

The unusual combination of flavors in this recipe will surprise and delight you.

Use a very sharp knife to cut a slit into the flesh along the thickest side of each chicken breast half.

Dip the chicken breast halves in beaten egg and then in the breadcrumbs. Sear them in oil in a preheated browning dish.

MICROTIPS

Apricots

Because apricots are very rich in vitamins it is a good idea to make them part of your diet all year round. In winter, when fresh apricots are not available, you can use them in their dried form. If you find them tough, try soaking them in a little water in a covered bowl for 10 hours. To help prevent constipation, eat a mixture of soaked apricots and prunes with a little of the water in which they have soaked for breakfast each morning.

Drink Plenty of Water

It is impossible to overstate the importance of large quantities of water in a healthy diet. Although we absorb some water indirectly from such foods as vegetables, rice, cheese and milk, it is still important to drink several glasses of water each day. Water is absorbed quickly into the body by the small intestine and the blood carries it to other cells, bringing them nutrients and hastening the elimination of waste products.

Mineral Water

Mineral water is free from harmful bacteria and rich in such minerals as carbonates, calcium sulphate, bromine, iron and iodine. However, because of its high mineral content, it is not wise to drink too much. It is also not a good idea to drink too much artificially carbonated water. It frequently contains chemical additives and an excess of carbon dioxide, which may stimulate the gastric juices but which may also cause the stomach to become bloated.

MICROTIPS

For a Healthy Diet . . .

Healthy Snacks

When your stomach has a craving for food and you don't know what to eat, try raw carrots or celery sticks. Always have them in the refrigerator, ready for that moment when hunger strikes. Or, for a change, try nibbling on strips of red pepper, which makes a refreshing treat.

At snack time, make a habit of avoiding sugar —including the sugar in chewing gum and in fruit-flavored drinks. For one thing, too much sugar is full of empty calories and is simply not good for you and, for another, you are less likely to brush your teeth after a snack.

If you really can't resist something sweet, at least steer clear of caramels and fizzy drinks and instead choose fresh fruit, an unsweetened fruit drink, a fruit sorbet, yoghurt or a muffin made with wheat germ.

Watch Out for Hidden Salt

Beware of consuming too much salt. Most of us eat more than we need, often without noticing its presence in our food. The nuts you eat at snack time, chosen instead of the potato chips that have no nutritional value, may contain a surprising amount of salt.

Know the Difference between Butter and Margarine

In spite of what many people think, butter does not have more calories than margarine. In fact, they both contain roughly the same quantity. The difference between the two lies instead in the type of fat used to make each. Butter contains animal fat whereas margarine contains mainly vegetable fat—a useful bit of information for those with high cholesterol counts!

Beware of Hidden Sugar

Watch out for hidden sugar. It's easy to see just how much you are putting in your coffee but not so easy to judge the amount in cakes, jams, sweetened drinks, fruit-flavored jellies and fruit yoghurts, all of which you may eat quite regularly.

Tofu: An Excellent Source of Protein

Tofu is a cheesy substance made from soy milk. It is an excellent source of protein and therefore an asset to healthy eating. It has, however, a rather bland taste and is best used in recipes that include complementary spices and condiments.

Chicken with Mushrooms

Level of Difficulty	
Preparation Time	15 min
Cost per Serving	$
Number of Servings	4
Nutritional Value	360 calories 17.4 g protein 0.9 mg iron
Food Exchanges	3 oz meat 1/4 milk exchange 3 fat exchanges
Cooking Time	14 min
Standing Time	None
Power Level	100%
Write Your Cooking Time Here	

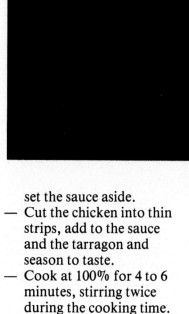

Ingredients

500 mL (2 cups) chicken
breast, cooked
125 mL (1/2 cup)
mushrooms, thinly sliced
50 mL (1/4 cup) butter
15 mL (1 tablespoon) green
onion, finely chopped
50 mL (1/4 cup) flour
250 mL (1 cup) 2% milk
250 mL (1 cup) chicken stock
5 mL (1 teaspoon) tarragon
salt and pepper to taste

Method

— Put the butter in a dish and
melt at 100% for 1
minute.
— Add the green onion and
flour and mix well.
— Add the milk and the
chicken stock, stirring
thoroughly.
— Cook at 100% for 5 to 7
minutes, stirring twice
during the cooking time.
— Add the mushrooms and
set the sauce aside.
— Cut the chicken into thin
strips, add to the sauce
and the tarragon and
season to taste.
— Cook at 100% for 4 to 6
minutes, stirring twice
during the cooking time.

MICROTIPS

Rice: White, Brown or Semi-Cooked

The difference between white rice and brown rice is that white rice has been hulled, or polished, to remove the outer bran layer and the germ from the grain. This process may refine the taste and texture but it robs the grain of several nutrients.

Brown rice, on the other hand, retains its bran layer and germ and therefore has a nutty flavor and crunchy texture that many people enjoy. Although it takes longer to cook than polished white rice, it has more nutritional value.

Semi-cooked (frequently referred to as "converted") rice is a compromise between white rice and brown rice. It is pressure cooked before it is hulled, the steam forcing some of the nutrients from the outer bran layer into the grain itself. It is then hulled. This type of rice is a little darker than white rice but it is more nourishing and has a similar texture.

Veal Escallops with Mushrooms and Wine

Level of Difficulty	🍴🍴
Preparation Time	20 min
Cost per Serving	$ $
Number of Servings	4
Nutritional Value	444 calories 40 g protein 4.3 mg iron
Food Exchanges	5 oz meat 1 vegetable exchange 1-1/2 fat exchanges
Cooking Time	13 min
Standing Time	4 min
Power Level	100%, 70%
Write Your Cooking Time Here	

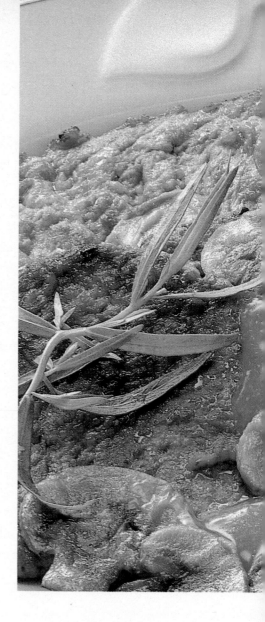

Ingredients
4 veal escallops, 115 g (4 oz) each
1 egg, beaten
150 mL (2/3 cup) Parmesan cheese, grated
30 mL (2 tablespoons) butter
1 284 mL (10 oz) can sliced mushrooms
5 mL (1 teaspoon) powdered chicken concentrate
1 mL (1/4 teaspoon) garlic powder
50 mL (1/4 cup) Marsala wine or white wine
15 mL (1 tablespoon) cornstarch
45 mL (3 tablespoons) cold water

Method
— Place the veal escallops between 2 sheets of waxed paper and pound them with a meat mallet until they are 3 mm (1/8 inch) thick.
— Dip the escallops in the beaten egg and then coat them with the Parmesan cheese.
— Preheat a browning dish at 100% for 7 minutes, add the butter and heat at 100% for 30 seconds.
— Sear the escallops and add the mushrooms; cover and set aside.
— In a bowl combine the powdered chicken concentrate, garlic powder and Marsala (or white) wine and pour the mixture over the escallops.
— Cover and cook at 70% for 5 minutes.
— Rearrange the escallops so that those in the center of the dish are now turned toward the outer edge. Turn the escallops over.
— Cover again and continue to cook at 70% for 4 to 6

minutes longer.
— Dissolve the cornstarch in the water and add to the liquid in the veal dish.
— Heat at 70% for 1 to 2 minutes, or until the sauce thickens, stirring once during the cooking time.
— Allow to stand for 4 minutes before serving.

Place the escallops between 2 sheets of waxed paper and pound them with a mallet until they are 3 mm (1/3 inch) thick.

Pour the mixture of powdered chicken concentrate, garlic powder and Marsala (or white) wine over the seared escallops; cover and cook as directed in the recipe.

Mexican Beef Stew

Level of Difficulty	
Preparation Time	20 min
Cost per Serving	**$**
Number of Servings	4
Nutritional Value	293 calories 35 g protein 5.6 mg iron
Food Exchanges	3 oz meat 3 vegetable exchanges
Cooking Time	27 min
Standing Time	4 min
Power Level	100%
Write Your Cooking Time Here	

Ingredients
450 g (1 lb) lean ground beef
2 onions, chopped
2 cloves garlic, chopped
2 sticks celery, chopped
2 carrots, thinly sliced
250 mL (1 cup) beef stock
1 zucchini, thinly sliced
125 mL (1/2 cup) whole corn kernels
30 mL (2 tablespoons) red pepper, chopped
1 796 mL (28 oz) can tomatoes, chopped
15 mL (1 tablespoon) chili powder
5 mL (1 teaspoon) cayenne pepper

Method
— Put the onions, garlic, celery and carrots in a dish and add 50 mL (1/4 cup) of the beef stock.
— Cover and cook at 100% for 7 to 9 minutes, stirring once during the cooking time.
— Add the ground beef and cook at 100% for 5 to 7 minutes, stirring twice with a fork to break up the meat.
— Add all the other ingredients and mix well.
— Cover and cook at 100% for 9 to 11 minutes, stirring twice during the cooking time.
— Allow to stand for 4 minutes before serving.

Add the ground beef to the mixture of onions, garlic, celery, carrots and beef stock and cook at 100% for 5 to 7 minutes.

Add all the other ingredients, mix well and complete the final stage of cooking.

MICROTIPS

A Crunchy Mexican Treat

Add an authentic Mexican touch by serving this beef stew with corn chips to dip in the sauce.

Beef Sauté with Orange Segments

Level of Difficulty	⅃ㅣ
Preparation Time	20 min*
Cost per Serving	$
Number of Servings	4
Nutritional Value	322 calories 28.4 g protein 5.8 mg iron
Food Exchanges	3 oz meat 2 vegetable exchanges 1 fruit exchange
Cooking Time	7 min
Standing Time	4 min
Power Level	100%, 70%
Write Your Cooking Time Here	

MICROTIPS

Preserving the Vitamin C in Oranges

When buying oranges, select those with firm, smooth, finely textured skin. This type of skin protects the pulp from drying out, keeping your oranges juicier.

As Vitamin C oxidizes very quickly when exposed to the air, you should try to prepare fresh orange juice just before you drink it.

* The meat should be left to marinate for 1 hour before cooking.

Ingredients
450 g (1 lb) sirloin tip beef
50 mL (1/4 cup) soy sauce
125 mL (1/2 cup) orange juice
1 mL (1/4 teaspoon) ginger
1 mL (1/4 teaspoon) garlic powder
30 mL (2 tablespoons) oil
1 onion, thinly sliced
500 mL (2 cups) snow peas
250 mL (1 cup) mushrooms, thinly sliced
1 green pepper, thinly sliced
30 mL (2 tablespoons) cornstarch
1 284 mL (10 oz) can orange segments

Method
— Pound the beef with a mallet until it is quite thin and cut it into strips.
— In a dish combine the soy sauce, orange juice, ginger and garlic powder; add the strips of beef to the mixture and allow to marinate for 1 hour, stirring several times.
— Preheat a browning dish at 100% for 7 minutes.
— While the dish is heating remove the meat from the marinade; pat dry and reserve the marinade.
— Pour the oil into the browning dish and heat at 100% for 30 seconds.
— Sear the beef and remove it from the dish.
— Heat the browning dish again, at 100% for 4 minutes.
— Sauté the vegetables.
— Add the meat; cover and cook at 70% for 4 to 5 minutes, stirring once.
— Dissolve the cornstarch in the marinade and pour it over the mixture.
— Cook at 100% for 1 to 2 minutes, or until the mixture thickens, stirring once during the cooking time.
— Add the orange segments; cover and allow to stand for 4 minutes before serving.

Lamb Chops with Beans

Level of Difficulty	🍴
Preparation Time	15 min*
Cost per Serving	$ $
Number of Servings	4
Nutritional Value	495 calories 16.9 g protein 6.3 mg iron
Food Exchanges	5 oz meat 1 vegetable exchange 1 bread exchange
Cooking Time	1 h 57 min
Standing Time	None
Power Level	100%, 70%, 50%
Write Your Cooking Time Here	🍎✏️

* The beans must be left to soak in cold water for 12 hours before cooking.

Ingredients
8 lamb chops
250 mL (1 cup) dried navy beans
1 398 mL (14 oz) can tomatoes, chopped (including their liquid)
2 cloves garlic, thinly sliced
30 mL (2 tablespoons) lemon juice
5 mL (1 teaspoon) lemon zest
2 mL (1/2 teaspoon) basil
1 mL (1/4 teaspoon) thyme
30 mL (2 tablespoons) parsley, chopped
pepper to taste

Method
— Put the beans in a dish and leave them to soak in cold water for 12 hours.
— Drain the beans and put them back in the dish; cover with hot water.
— Cover and cook at 100% for 30 minutes.
— Stir the beans, reduce the power level to 50% and cook for 1 hour, or until the beans are soft but not mushy.
— Drain the beans and add the tomatoes and their liquid, the garlic, lemon juice, lemon zest, basil and thyme.
— Increase the power level to 100% and cook for 14 to 16 minutes, stirring once during the cooking time, and set aside.
— Arrange the lamb chops in a shallow baking dish, the thicker parts facing the outside.
— Reduce the power level to 70% and cook for 5 minutes.

— Turn the chops over, arranging them in such a way that the thicker parts are still toward the outside of the dish.
— Continue to cook at 70% for 4 to 6 minutes.
— Sprinkle the chops with parsley and pepper.
— Reheat the beans and serve with the lamb chops.

To ensure that the lamb chops cook properly, arrange them so that the thicker parts face the outside of the dish.

After they have cooked for 5 minutes turn the chops over, arranging them in such a way that the thicker parts are still facing the outside of the dish.

Mexican-Style Pita Sandwich

Level of Difficulty	🍴🔪
Preparation Time	20 min
Cost per Serving	$
Number of Servings	4
Nutritional Value	319 calories 34.4 g protein 4.1 mg iron
Food Exchanges	3 oz meat 1 vegetable exchange 1 bread exchange
Cooking Time	9 min
Standing Time	None
Power Level	100%
Write Your Cooking Time Here	

Ingredients
340 g (12 oz) lean ground beef
125 mL (1/2 cup) onion,
finely chopped
2 cloves garlic, crushed
125 mL (1/2 cup) green
pepper, chopped
175 mL (3/4 cup) tomato
juice
5 mL (1 teaspoon) crushed red
chili peppers (or less)
125 mL (1/2 cup) mozzarella
cheese, grated
salt and pepper to taste
4 whole wheat pita pockets,
cut into two

Method
— Put the ground beef in a
dish and cook at 100% for
4 to 5 minutes, stirring
twice during the cooking
time to break up the meat.
— Drain off any fat and add
the onion, garlic and
green pepper; cook at
100% for 2 minutes,
stirring once during the
cooking time.
— Add the tomato juice and
the crushed chili peppers.
— Season to taste, add the
mozzarella and mix well.

— Fill each pita pocket with
an equal amount of the
mixture.
— Put 4 pita halves on a
plate; cover and heat at
100% for 1 minute.
— Repeat this step with the
remaining 4 halves.

In less than 30 minutes you can transform these few ingredients into a snack suitable for any occasion.

MICROTIPS

Chili Powder and Chili Peppers

Chili powder, based on various blends of spices including cumin, coriander, cayenne, tumeric, paprika and sweet or hot peppers, is much used in Central and South American cooking. Chili peppers, which are available dried and crushed, are known for their potent addition of heat to these dishes. These seasoning agents are the ones that give the recipes for Mexican Beef Stew (page 66) and Mexican-Style Pita Sandwich (page 72, opposite) their distinctive flavors. Be sure to adjust the amount of these ingredients in such recipes to suit your own taste.

Tuna Florentine

Level of Difficulty	🍴
Preparation Time	20 min
Cost per Serving	$
Number of Servings	4
Nutritional Value	344 calories 23.1 g protein 3 mg iron
Food Exchanges	2.5 oz meat 2 vegetable exchanges 1 bread exchange 1 fat exchange
Cooking Time	23 min
Standing Time	3 min
Power Level	100%
Write Your Cooking Time Here	

Ingredients
1 213 mL (7-1/2 oz) can tuna, drained
30 mL (2 tablespoons) butter
1 onion, thinly sliced
1 clove garlic, crushed
250 mL (1 cup) tomatoes, chopped and drained
250 mL (1 cup) tomato sauce
2 mL (1/2 teaspoon) basil
2 mL (1/2 teaspoon) sugar
2 mL (1/2 teaspoon) oregano
salt and pepper to taste
1 284 g (10 oz) package fresh spinach
115 g (4 oz) egg noodles, cooked
50 mL (1/4 cup) Parmesan cheese, grated

Method
— Put the butter, onion and garlic in a dish and cook at 100% for 1 to 2 minutes.
— Add the tomates, tomato sauce, basil, sugar and oregano; season to taste and cook at 100% for 9 to 12 minutes, stirring once during the cooking time.
— Use a fork to break up the tomatoes and set the mixture aside.
— Wash and drain the spinach, put in a dish and cook covered at 100% for 3 to 4 minutes.
— Using a sieve, drain the spinach well and chop finely.

— Add the cooked noodles and the tuna to the tomato sauce and place the mixture in the center of a casserole.
— Arrange the spinach around the tuna, noodle and tomato mixture and sprinkle with Parmesan cheese.
— Cook at 100% for 4 to 5 minutes, giving the dish a half-turn halfway through the cooking time.
— Allow to stand for 3 minutes before serving.

This easy-to-make dish features tuna, spinach and tomatoes.

Add the tuna to the sauce and then add to the cooked noodles. Pour the mixture into the center of a casserole dish.

Arrange the spinach around the tuna, noodle and tomato mixture and sprinkle with Parmesan cheese. Then complete the final stage of cooking.

Shrimp Risotto

Level of Difficulty	
Preparation Time	15 min
Cost per Serving	$ $
Number of Servings	4
Nutritional Value	168 calories 24.4 g protein 2.5 mg iron
Food Exchanges	3 oz meat 1 bread exchange 1 vegetable exchange
Cooking Time	19 min
Standing Time	8 min
Power Level	100%, 70%
Write Your Cooking Time Here	

Ingredients
450 g (1 lb) shrimp, shelled and cooked
250 mL (1 cup) long grain rice
500 mL (2 cups) hot chicken stock
1 green pepper, diced
1 red pepper, thinly sliced
250 mL (1 cup) mushrooms, thinly sliced
a few drops Tabasco sauce
15 mL (1 tablespoon) lemon juice
salt and pepper to taste

Method
— Put the rice in a dish and add the chicken stock.
— Cover and cook at 100% for 5 minutes; reduce the power level to 70% and continue to cook for 10 more minutes.
— Stir the rice and add the green and red peppers and the mushrooms; cover and allow to stand for 5 minutes.
— Add the cooked shrimp, Tabasco sauce and lemon juice; season to taste.
— Heat at 100% for 3 to 4 minutes, stirring once during the cooking time.
— Cover and allow to stand for 3 minutes before serving.

Scallops with Lemon and Spinach

Level of Difficulty	
Preparation Time	20 min*
Cost per Serving	$ $
Number of Servings	4
Nutritional Value	199 calories 23.2 g protein 3.7 mg iron
Food Exchanges	2 oz meat 1 vegetable exchange 1-1/2 fat exchanges
Cooking Time	16 min
Standing Time	3 min
Power Level	100%, 70%
Write Your Cooking Time Here	

* The scallops must be left in the refrigerator to soak in the milk for 8 hours before cooking.

Ingredients
340 g (12 oz) scallops, cut into two
250 mL (1 cup) milk
30 mL (2 tablespoons) butter
2 green onions, thinly sliced
1 clove garlic, crushed
15 mL (1 tablespoon) flour
salt and pepper to taste
15 mL (1 tablespoon) lemon juice
5 mL (1 teaspoon) lemon zest
1 284 g (10 oz) package fresh spinach

Method
— Put the scallops in a dish and add the milk; leave to soak for 8 hours in the refrigerator.
— Drain the scallops and reserve the milk.
— Put the butter, green onion and garlic in a dish and cook at 100% for 2 minutes, stirring once during the cooking time.
— Add the flour and mix well.
— Add the reserved milk and cook at 100% for 3 to 4 minutes, stirring twice during the cooking time.
— Season to taste and set aside.
— Put the scallops in another dish and add the lemon juice and lemon zest; cover and cook at 70% for 2 to 3 minutes, stirring once during the cooking time.
— Leave the dish covered and allow to stand for 3 minutes.

- Wash and drain the
  spinach and put it into a
  dish; cover and cook at
  100% for 3 to 4 minutes.
- Drain the spinach and
  chop it.
- Line a shallow dish with
  the spinach and place the
  scallops on top.
- Cover with the sauce and
  heat at 100% for 2 to 3
  minutes before serving.

*This delicious scallop recipe will
delight your guests. Here are
the ingredients that should be
assembled before you begin to
prepare it.*

*Line a dish with the spinach,
place the scallops on top, and
pour the sauce over the
assembled dish. Heat through
at 100% for 2 to 3 minutes.*

Fisherman's Stew

Level of Difficulty	🍴
Preparation Time	20 min
Cost per Serving	$ $
Number of Servings	6
Nutritional Value	371 calories 37.7 g protein 2.5 mg iron
Food Exchanges	3 oz meat 1/2 milk exchange 1 bread exchange 1 fat exchange
Cooking Time	19 min
Standing Time	None
Power Level	100%
Write Your Cooking Time Here	

Ingredients
175 mL (3/4 cup) shrimp, cooked
425 mL (1-3/4 cups) salmon, cooked
250 mL (1 cup) potatoes, peeled and cubed
1 onion, sliced
125 mL (1/2 cup) celery, diced
75 mL (1/3 cup) hot water
250 mL (1 cup) tomatoes, chopped and drained
2 mL (1/2 teaspoon) thyme
10 mL (2 teaspoons) dried parsley
1 mL (1/4 teaspoon) celery seed
salt and pepper to taste
30 mL (2 tablespoons) butter
30 mL (2 tablespoons) flour
500 mL (2 cups) 2% milk

Method
— Put the potatoes, onion and celery in a dish and add the hot water; cover and cook at 100% for 5 to 7 minutes, stirring once during the cooking time.
— Add the tomatoes, cover again and cook at 100% for 3 to 4 minutes, stirring once during the cooking time.
— Add the thyme, parsley and celery seed and season to taste.
— Add the shrimp and salmon; cover and set aside.
— Melt the butter in a dish at 100% for 45 seconds.
— Add the flour and mix well.
— Add the milk and cook at 100% for 5 to 7 minutes, stirring twice during the cooking time.
— Pour the sauce over the shrimp and salmon mixture. Adjust the seasoning and reheat if necessary before serving.

Here are most of the ingredients you need to assemble before making this succulent dish. It is one that is bound to delight your guests.

Cook the potato, onion and celery at 100% for 5 to 7 minutes. Add the tomatoes and continue to cook as directed and then add the cooked shrimp and salmon.

Pour the sauce over the shrimp, salmon and vegetables and adjust the seasoning before serving.

81

Shrimp with Feta Cheese in Tomato Sauce

Level of Difficulty	▯▮▯
Preparation Time	20 min
Cost per Serving	$ $
Number of Servings	4
Nutritional Value	441 calories 30 g protein 3.1 mg iron
Food Exchanges	4 oz meat 2 vegetable exchanges 2 fat exchanges
Cooking Time	24 min
Standing Time	3 min
Power Level	100%
Write Your Cooking Time Here	

Ingredients
450 g (1 lb) shrimp, shelled
15 mL (1 tablespoon) oil
250 mL (1 cup) onion, chopped
2 cloves garlic, chopped
500 mL (2 cups) tomato sauce
30 mL (2 tablespoons) dry white vermouth
1 bay leaf
5 mL (1 teaspoon) oregano
pinch basil
175 mL (3/4 cup) black olives
175 g (6 oz) feta cheese, diced
salt and pepper to taste

Method
— Pour the oil into a dish and add the onion and garlic; cover and cook at 100% for 3 to 4 minutes, stirring once during the cooking time.
— Add the tomato sauce, vermouth, bay leaf, oregano and basil.
— Cook at 100% for 10 to 12 minutes, stirring once during the cooking time.
— Stir in the shrimp and continue to cook at 100% for 4 to 5 minutes, stirring once during the cooking time.
— Add the black olives and feta cheese and season to taste.
— Cook at 100% for 2 to 3 minutes.
— Stir gently, cover, and allow to stand for 3 minutes before serving.

This exotic dish will delight shrimp lovers. Begin by assembling these ingredients.

Stir the sauce once during the cooking time to ensure that it has a smooth consistency.

Add the black olives and the feta cheese just before the final stage of cooking.

Manicotti with Spinach

Level of Difficulty	
Preparation Time	20 min
Cost per Serving	**$**
Number of Servings	4
Nutritional Value	224 calories 16.7 g protein 2.9 mg iron
Food Exchanges	1 oz meat 2 vegetable exchanges 1 bread exchange
Cooking Time	31 min
Standing Time	5 min
Power Level	100%, 70%
Write Your Cooking Time Here	

Ingredients
8 manicotti
1 L (4 cups) boiling water

Sauce:
1 156 mL (5-1/2 oz) can tomato paste
250 mL (1 cup) water
1 clove garlic, chopped
1 mL (1/4 teaspoon) basil
1 mL (1/4 teaspoon) oregano
50 mL (1/4 cup) onion, finely chopped
salt and pepper to taste

Filling:
1 284 g (10 oz) package fresh spinach
250 mL (1 cup) cottage cheese
50 mL (1/4 cup) Parmesan cheese, grated

Method
— Pour the boiling water into a rectangular dish and add the manicotti.
— Cover and cook at 100% for 5 to 7 minutes.
— Drain the manicotti, rinse under cold water and set aside.
— Make the sauce by putting all the ingredients into a dish and mixing them well.
— Cook at 100% for 7 to 9 minutes, stirring once during the cooking time, and set aside.
— Finally, put the spinach into a dish; cover and cook at 100% for 4 to 5 minutes.
— Drain the spinach well and chop it finely.
— Mix the spinach with the cottage cheese and the Parmesan cheese.
— Stuff the manicotti with equal quantities of the spinach and cheese filling; arrange in a rectangular

baking dish and top with the sauce.
— Cook at 70% for 8 to 10 minutes, giving the dish a half-turn halfway through the cooking time.
— Allow to stand for 5 minutes before serving.

MICROTIPS

The Professional Approach

You probably have a piping bag somewhere in your kitchen. It can be used with a number of tips of varying sizes and shapes. The piping bag is frequently used for cake decorating, but it is also the perfect tool for stuffing pasta quickly and efficiently.

Desserts

Think of all the marvelous classic desserts in European cookery—Charlotte Russe, Mocha Cake with Chantilly Cream, Chocolate Cake, Black Forest Cake, Gâteau Saint-Honoré and such traditional Middle Eastern classics as Baklava drenched with honey—all wonderfully rich and delicious, bestowing international culinary reputations on the chefs who invented them. But however good they may be, these rich desserts are becoming more and more frowned upon by dietitians and people who are concerned about healthy eating. Still, if you really are a confirmed sugar addict, you can take comfort in the fact that moderate amounts of sugar will not do you too much harm.

What you must do is avoid excessive quantities of sugar. Large servings of rich desserts at every meal may well cause problems in terms of your health, not to mention your figure. Make it a rule not to eat more than one dessert each day.

One tip we can offer to help you avoid giving way to temptation is to include sufficient quantities of protein and other nutrients in all your meals. It is a well-known fact that a diet low in protein can leave you with an insatiable craving for sugar.

Desserts do not all get the same poor ratings from dietitians. In fact, some highly nutritious foods make excellent desserts; try a juicy apple, a cheese muffin or an oatmeal cookie with a glass of milk. Even pies and cakes vary in their nutritional value. The Coconut Pie given on page 94 provides far more nutrients than the typical sugar pie with ice cream that you might order in any number of restaurants.

All the desserts offered in the following pages do contain nutritional value worthy of mention. They include healthy ingredients, chosen from the major food groups—fruit, cereals such as rice and oats, and dairy products such as yoghurt and cheese being among them. All these ingredients contribute to tasty dessert preparations and can be justified in terms of healthy, well-balanced eating habits.

Whether you make healthy desserts because you want to or because you feel obligated to, you will find that they really are pleasant and do not leave you feeling deprived. Healthy cooking is quite delicious in its own right!

Cheese Muffins

Level of Difficulty	🍴
Preparation Time	15 min
Cost per Serving	**$**
Number of Servings	12
Nutritional Value	160 calories 15 g carbohydrate 8.1 g lipids
Food Exchanges	1 oz meat 1 bread exchange 1 fat exchange
Cooking Time	2 x 2 min
Standing Time	2 x 2 min
Power Level	90%
Write Your Cooking Time Here	

Ingredients
250 mL (1 cup) cheddar cheese, finely grated
425 mL (1-3/4 cups) whole wheat flour
15 mL (1 tablespoon) baking powder
2 mL (1/2 teaspoon) salt
30 mL (2 tablespoons) sugar
1 egg
175 mL (3/4 cup) skim milk
50 mL (1/4 cup) oil
30 mL (2 tablespoons) crumbled graham wafers

Method
— Combine the flour, baking powder, salt and sugar; add the cheddar cheese and set aside.
— In another bowl beat the egg and blend in the milk and oil.
— Make a well in the center of the dry ingredients and add the egg, milk and oil mixture.
— Stir just enough to moisten the dry ingredients.
— Line a 6 cup muffin pan with size 75 paper cases.
— Pour equal amounts of the batter into each muffin case, taking care to fill them just two thirds full.
— Sprinkle the batter in each muffin case with the graham wafer crumbs.
— Place the pan on a rack in the microwave oven and cook at 90% for 1-1/4 to 2 minutes, giving the pan a half-turn halfway through the cooking time.
— Allow to stand for 2 minutes.
— Repeat this procedure for the remaining 6 muffins.

These muffins are perfect for snacks, at breakfast or as a dessert. First assemble all the ingredients.

Make a well in the center of the mixture of flour, baking powder, salt and sugar and add the blended liquid ingredients. Stir just enough to moisten the dry ingredients.

Pour an equal quantity of the batter into each of the muffin cups, taking care to fill them just two thirds full. Top with the graham wafer crumbs and then cook the muffins.

Apple and Raisin Cake

Level of Difficulty	🍴
Preparation Time	15 min
Cost per Serving	$
Number of Servings	8
Nutritional Value	133 calories 20 g carbohydrate 6 g lipids
Food Exchanges	1 fruit exchange 1 bread exchange
Cooking Time	6 min
Standing Time	5 min
Power Level	70%
Write Your Cooking Time Here	

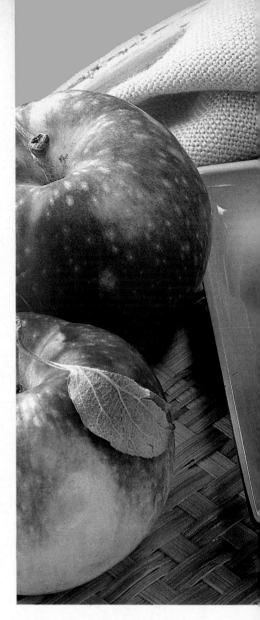

Ingredients
500 mL (2 cups) apples, peeled and grated
75 mL (1/3 cup) raisins
75 mL (1/3 cup) whole wheat flour
10 mL (2 teaspoons) baking powder
pinch salt
2 mL (1/2 teaspoon) cinnamon
0.5 mL (1/8 teaspoon) nutmeg
50 mL (1/4 cup) nuts, chopped
3 eggs, beaten
50 mL (1/4 cup) brown sugar, well packed

Method
— Combine the flour, baking powder, salt, cinnamon, nutmeg, nuts and raisins in a large bowl.
— In another bowl combine the beaten eggs, brown sugar and grated apple; add to the dry ingredients and mix well.
— Grease a 22.5 cm (9 inch) pie plate and pour the batter into it.
— Press the surface of the batter down gently to remove any air bubbles.
— Put the pie plate on a rack in the oven and cook at 70% for 4 to 6 minutes, giving the dish a half-turn halfway through the cooking time.
— Allow to stand for 5 minutes to finish cooking.

This recipe uses everyday ingredients but the finished cake is unusual and appealing.

Put the plate on a rack in the oven and cook at 70% for 4 to 6 minutes, giving the plate a half-turn halfway through the cooking time.

MICROTIPS

Making Healthy Muffins

Make your muffins healthier by replacing some or all of the white flour with whole wheat flour. Use 225 mL (7/8 cup) of whole wheat flour to replace 250 mL (1 cup) of white flour. You can also increase the amount of food fiber as well as the mineral quantity by adding wheat germ or bran.

Peaches Stuffed with Almonds and Raisins

Level of Difficulty	🍴🍴
Preparation Time	20 min
Cost per Serving	$ $
Number of Servings	4
Nutritional Value	225 calories 29.7 g carbohydrate 13.4 mg Vitamin C
Food Exchanges	3 fruit exchanges 1 fat exchange
Cooking Time	7 min
Standing Time	2 min
Power Level	100%, 70%
Write Your Cooking Time Here	

Ingredients
4 good quality peaches
500 mL (2 cups) boiling water
50 mL (1/4 cup) orange juice
30 mL (2 tablespoons) butter
50 mL (1/4 cup) almonds, sliced
50 mL (1/4 cup) raisins
pinch cinnamon
30 mL (2 tablespoons) liquid honey
15 mL (1 tablespoon) brandy

Method
— Put the peaches into the boiling water for 1 minute and remove them.
— Peel the peaches and cut them in half, removing the pit.
— Arrange the peach halves in a dish, sprinkle them with orange juice, and set aside.
— Melt the butter in a bowl at 100% for 30 seconds; add the almonds and cook at 100% for 2 to 3 minutes, stirring once halfway through the cooking time.
— Add the raisins and mix well.
— Fill the center cavity of each peach half with this mixture and sprinkle with cinnamon.
— Pour a little honey over each peach half and sprinkle with brandy.
— Cover the dish and cook at 70% for 3 to 4 minutes, or until the peaches are tender, giving the dish a half-turn after the first 2 minutes.
— Allow to stand for 2 minutes before serving.

You can put these ingredients together in less than 30 minutes to make a wonderfully spicy dessert.

Put the peaches into boiling water for 1 minute and remove them. Peel the peaches, cut them in half, and remove the pits.

Fill the center cavity of each peach half with the mixture of nuts and raisins and sprinkle with cinnamon. Add the honey and brandy and cook as directed.

93

Coconut Pie

Level of Difficulty	🍴
Preparation Time	10 min
Cost per Serving	**$**
Number of Servings	6
Nutritional Value	163 calories 22 g carbohydrate 7.1 g lipids
Food Exchanges	1 fruit exchange 1 bread exchange 1 fat exchange
Cooking Time	8 min
Standing Time	5 min
Power Level	70%
Write Your Cooking Time Here	✏️🍎

Ingredients
250 mL (1 cup) coconut, shredded and toasted
2 eggs, beaten
250 mL (1 cup) skim milk
75 mL (1/3 cup) sugar
50 mL (1/4 cup) flour
5 mL (1 teaspoon) melted butter
2 mL (1/2 teaspoon) baking powder
5 mL (1 teaspoon) vanilla essence

Method
— Put all the ingredients together in a bowl and mix well.
— Grease a 20 cm (8 inch) pie plate and add the mixture.
— Place the plate on a rack in the oven and cook at 70% for 6 to 8 minutes, giving the plate a half-turn halfway through the cooking time.
— Allow to stand for 5 minutes to finish off the cooking.

Assemble all the ingredients for this recipe and you will be just minutes away from having a dessert that will delight your guests.

Give the plate a half-turn halfway through the cooking time to ensure even cooking.

MICROTIPS

Low-Cost Desserts

It is a good idea to use powdered skim milk if you want to eat healthily and economically at the same time. If you keep a liter of reconstituted skim milk on hand in your refrigerator to use in desserts and sauces, you will be able to make quite a saving. Cooked dishes that use reconstituted skim milk have the same taste and nutritional value as dishes cooked with regular skim milk. The only difference is in the cost!

Low-Calorie Desserts

Think about this fact: a one-crust pie contains almost 100 calories less than a two-crust pie!

Creamed Rice with Peaches

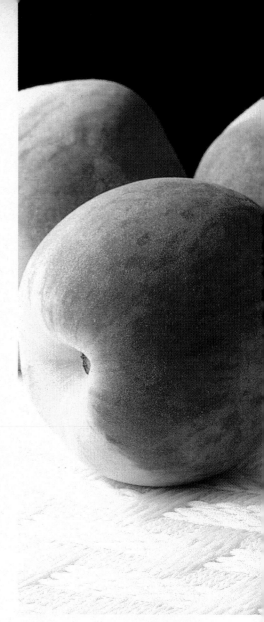

Level of Difficulty	🍴
Preparation Time	10 min
Cost per Serving	**$**
Number of Servings	2
Nutritional Value	163 calories 27 g carbohydrate 2.5 mg Vitamin C
Food Exchanges	1 fruit exchange 1/2 bread exchange
Cooking Time	10 min
Standing Time	3 min
Power Level	70%
Write Your Cooking Time Here	

Ingredients
125 mL (1/2 cup) cooked rice
125 mL (1/2 cup) peaches, coarsely chopped
1 egg
175 mL (3/4 cup) skim milk
1 mL (1/4 teaspoon) lemon juice
pinch nutmeg

Method
— Combine the rice and chopped peaches in a dish.
— In another bowl beat the egg and continue to beat as you add the milk and lemon juice.
— Pour the mixture over the rice and sprinkle with nutmeg.
— Place the dish on a rack in the oven and cook at 70% for 9 to 10 minutes, stirring every 4 minutes.
— Allow to stand for 3 minutes.

This lovely, creamy dessert can be made in less than 30 minutes and can be served hot or cold. First, assemble the necessary ingredients.

Combine the cooked rice and the chopped peaches.

Pour the mixture of egg, milk and lemon juice over the rice and peaches.

Place the dish on a rack in the oven and cook at 70% for 9 to 10 minutes, stirring every 4 minutes during the cooking time.

Oatmeal Cookies

Level of Difficulty	🍴
Preparation Time	15 min
Cost per Serving	$
Number of Servings	36 cookies (18 servings)
Nutritional Value*	145 calories 25.1 g carbohydrate 4.4 g lipids
Food Exchanges*	1 fruit exchange 1 bread exchange
Cooking Time	1-1/2 x 3 min
Standing Time	2 x 3 min
Power Level	90%
Write Your Cooking Time Here	

* Calculations are for two cookies.

Ingredients
500 mL (2 cups) rolled oats
50 mL (1/4 cup) oil
125 mL (1/2 cup) brown sugar
2 eggs
250 mL (1 cup) raisins
45 mL (3 tablespoons) molasses
425 mL (1-3/4 cups) flour
5 mL (1 teaspoon) baking soda
5 mL (1 teaspoon) salt
5 mL (1 teaspoon) cinnamon
5 mL (1 teaspoon) baking powder

Method
— Combine the oil and brown sugar in a bowl.
— Add the eggs, one at a time, and then blend in the rolled oats and raisins.
— Add the remaining ingredients, stirring constantly.
— Arrange 12 portions of 5 mL (1 teaspoon) each on a tray.
— Place the tray on a rack and cook at 90% for 1 to 1-1/2 minutes, giving the tray a half-turn halfway through the cooking time.
— Allow to stand for 2 minutes.
— Repeat this procedure twice more to make a total of 36 cookies.

Cranberry Bread

Level of Difficulty	🍴
Preparation Time	20 min
Cost per Serving	**$**
Number of Servings ·	about 10 slices
Nutritional Value	143 calories 23.5 g carbohydrate 8.2 mg Vitamin C
Food Exchanges	1 fruit exchange 1 bread exchange
Cooking Time	11 min
Standing Time	5 min
Power Level	70%
Write Your Cooking Time Here	

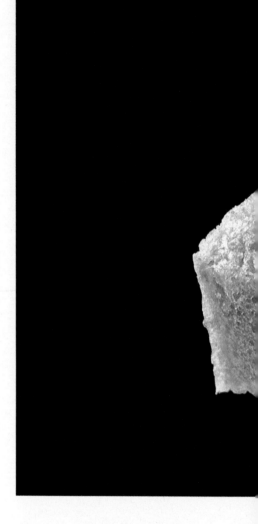

Ingredients
250 mL (1 cup) cranberry sauce
150 mL (2/3 cup) whole wheat flour
150 mL (2/3 cup) all purpose flour
10 mL (2 teaspoons) baking powder
2 mL (1/2 teaspoon) baking soda
5 mL (1 teaspoon) salt
30 mL (2 tablespoons) oil
2 eggs, beaten
175 mL (3/4 cup) unsweetened orange juice
15 mL (1 tablespoon) orange zest

Method
— Combine the two types of flour, the baking powder, baking soda and salt in a bowl.
— Put the oil, eggs, orange juice and orange zest in another bowl and mix well.
— Blend the wet ingredients with the dry; add the cranberry sauce and mix thoroughly.
— Grease a loaf pan and add the mixture.
— Shield the ends of the pan with strips of aluminum foil.
— Place the loaf on a rack in the oven and cook at 70% for 9 to 11 minutes, giving the dish a half-turn and removing the strips of foil after the first 5 minutes.
— Allow to stand for 5 minutes to finish cooking.

This novel dessert is both delicious and easy to make. Here are the ingredients you should assemble before you begin to prepare it.

Blend the wet ingredients with the dry and mix well.

Add the cranberry sauce and mix thoroughly until smooth.

101

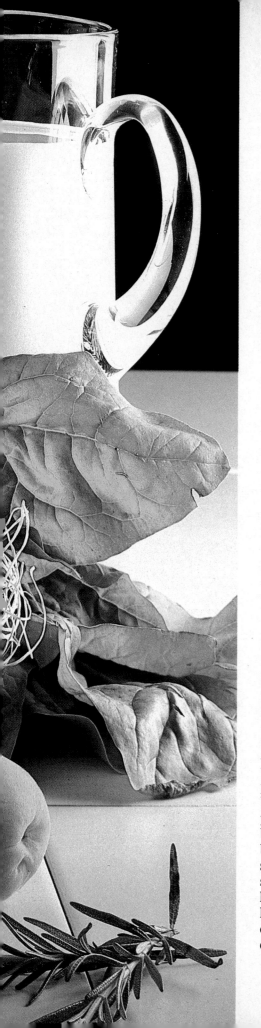

Meal Planning

Have you ever given any thought to the unbelievable variety of foods that nature provides for us? And are you the type of person who is always eager to try the latest exotic vegetable in the produce department? Or do you belong to the group that enjoys steak and French fries for lunch followed by spaghetti and meatballs for dinner one day and then the reverse on the following day?

You will enjoy your food all the more if you break away from this monotonous pattern. The temptation to have your meals in fast-food restaurants will diminish because, on changing your eating habits, the thought of having the same old meals will lose its appeal.

Try to vary your menu with the seasons. Enjoy strawberries in June, blueberries in August, asparagus in the spring and eggplant in the fall. And in the middle of winter, mandarins appear on the shelves in the green grocer shops and provide a little sunshine.

Add interest to your menu by varying the way in which you prepare certain foods. A boiled potato is simple to prepare and delicious to eat but quite different from a baked potato topped with a spoonful of plain yoghurt, served stuffed with corn or à la normande (sliced potatoes layered with sliced leeks and cooked in white veal stock or cream).

Experiment with the different fruits and vegetables you find in the produce department. The wide variety currently available to us is endless—there is more to life than McIntosh apples and carrots. Make it a habit to try new recipes, such as leeks vinaigrette or poached apricots.

Are you tired of sandwiches made with white bread? Other types of bread, such as pita pockets or Viennese loaf, are available to liven up your lunch.

You can find great variety at the meat counter as well. Take a break from the same old limited range of beef, pork and chicken. Try lamb, game and offal instead for a change.

Dry legumes are another good source of protein. Many different types of beans can be used to create colorful and unusual dishes with real nutritional value.

Try different color combinations, pleasing to both the eye and the palate. Enjoy sole meunière in a new way by serving it with spinach rather than cauliflower.

However, don't be totally swayed by the urge to create meals as colorful as a Renoir painting or as exotic as the mysterious East. Always remember to include dishes from the four main food groups in your menu for great tasting food that really is good for you!

Questions and Answers

What quantity of carbohydrates should I eat each day?

You should eat foods containing between 200 and and 250 grams of carbohydrates each day. It is not necessary to keep track of your intake if your diet is well balanced; your quota is easily achieved by including the proper amounts of whole wheat bread, dried fruit, rice or legumes, fruits, vegetables and dairy products.

Is it better to eat food raw or cooked?

The foods that nature provides contain, in their raw form, a balanced combination of nutrients. It is therefore a good idea to eat some raw foods each day. Try to begin each meal with a food that is not cooked, such as fruit, vegetables (crudités) or vegetable juice. One advantage to eating raw foods is that they do stimulate the digestive juices and therefore facilitate digestion.

Do all types of bread have the same nutritional value?

White bread is made with refined flour that is artificially enriched in an attempt to replace some of the nutrients lost in the refining process. It is no longer regarded as the best.

Today, whole wheat bread is preferred, but not all brown breads are the same. Those that are referred to as brown bread or cracked wheat bread are made from partly refined flour and colored with caramel or molasses. To qualify as whole wheat, bread must contain at least 60% whole wheat flour. Whole wheat bread is an excellent dietary source of fiber.

How can I prevent the loss of nutrients from foods?

Many foods tend to deteriorate over time, with a corresponding loss of nutrients. In many cases, excessive humidity or heat can lead to an even more rapid loss of nutritional quality. For example, if you leave an egg at room temperature for just one hour, it will deteriorate as much as it would over an entire day in the refrigerator.

Fruit juices quickly lose their Vitamin C content if they are exposed to the air and should therefore be stored in containers that are airtight.

The cooking process also destroys nutrients; precious vitamins are destroyed by heat and others are discarded with the cooking water. For this reason, microwave cooking is particularly effective. The problem of loss of nutritional value is minimized because this cooking method is very quick and requires very little water.

Are microwave ovens dangerous?

It has been proved beyond a doubt that, if the microwave oven is used in the correct manner, any food cooked or reheated in it will have a nutritional value equal to or greater than the same food cooked in the conventional way. The microwaves stimulate the molecules of water, fat and sugar that are found in nearly all foods. These molecules move vigorously and collide with each other when they are stimulated by microwave energy and, in so doing, create enough heat to cook the food quickly.

There is an important difference between microwaves and X-rays. Unlike X-rays, microwaves simply pass through the containers and their foods, leaving no traces of the waves behind nor altering the food in any hidden way. It is impossible to accidentally ingest microwaves because they do not remain in the food to be consumed.

How can I teach my children to eat properly?

You may have heard of a French teacher in Ontario who invited a student to try some traditional maple taffy. The student replied politely, "No thank you, I never eat candy." The moral of the story is quite clear; parents and other adults play an important role in teaching children what is good for them and what is not. A child who is raised to eat healthily is likely to learn good eating habits and to keep to them— as shown in the above example. The same child is also likely to take pleasure in preparing food and learning how to cook.

Also, it should be noted that microwave cooking is perfectly safe for children because, given the way in which the oven works, there is very little risk of the child getting burned. And that's a real plus!

Is it true that cheese is constipating?

No, cheese will not cause constipation if your diet is balanced and includes a sufficient quantity of fruits and vegetables. The food fiber they contain will keep the intestinal tract functioning properly, allowing the cheese to be absorbed by the body.

Vegetarianism and Natural Foods

In the West, vegetarianism has gained in popularity as a result of the movement advocating a "return to the land." There are, however, many other reasons why people choose this type of diet and most of them are valid.

As a general rule, people who choose vegetarianism are keen to improve their eating habits. But there are specific arguments that they use to support their point of view. For example, most types of meat, particularly red meats, contain a great deal of saturated animal fat, which can lead to high blood pressure. Also, some people claim that animals raised for slaughter are frequently fed and treated with chemicals that can accumulate in the body until they reach levels that are toxic.

Vegetarianism is preached by some for philosophical reasons. Hindus, for example, believe that in eating animal flesh the terror felt by the animal when it was slaughtered is also ingested. This belief is borne out to some extent by the scientific discovery that, at the point of death, the animal's body secretes an abundance of adrenaline.

There are also social reasons for choosing vegetarianism. An American best-seller published in 1971, titled *Diet for a Small Planet,* points out that cattle raised for slaughter must each consume at least 16 pounds (7.3 kilograms) of vegetable protein to produce one pound (454 grams) of meat. The author, Frances Moore Lappé, proposed a theory that was considered revolutionary at the time, namely, that famine in the Third World would be eliminated if needy people there were given the cereals that Americans squandered on raising cattle. The viability of this theory is still debated by politicians.

And, finally, vegetarianism is an economical way to eat. If you compare the price of sirloin steak with the price of tofu in ginger sauce, you would probably revise your grocery list in an instant.

Some Definitions of Vegetarianism

The number of misconceptions surrounding the word "vegetarianism" is notable. Vegetarianism, in the strict sense of the word, means the exclusion of all food of animal origin, including eggs and dairy products. But not all vegetarians adhere to this principle. Some people who call themselves vegetarians have simply eliminated red meat from their diets and regularly eat fish and poultry. And between these two schools of thought are those (ovo-vegetarians) who do not eat meat, poultry or fish but who do eat eggs and still others (lacto-ovo-vegetarians) who eat eggs and other dairy products as well.

Do We Need Meat?

For many people, meat plays such a major role in their diets that they would feel undernourished in some way if it were eliminated. However, food science has demonstrated that there are numerous other sources of protein. Eggs, for example, contain as much protein as beef. Also, cereals, nuts and legumes contain incomplete protein that can be eaten in combination with other foods to provide complete protein— protein of a quality as high as that found in meat, eggs and dairy products. These facts provide a strong case for vegetarianism. In fact, in recent years the food industry has adopted some of the special foods that vegetarians have promoted, such as carob, sesame seed and whole wheat pasta.

Vegetarianism with a Gourmet Touch

It is quite possible to be vegetarian and still enjoy good food. A wide range of delicious and exotic food that is vegetarian—known to

Health Food Terminology

satisfy the appetite and to provide the required nutrients and sufficient calories—is available. Besides, not all vegetarians are lanky eccentrics dressed in homespun cloth. There are people who enjoy vegetarian food all or some of the time, at all levels of society. They can tell you that eating a vegetarian meal is a sensory experience; the colors, the aromas and the textures provide a wonderful change from ordinary food.

If you are one of those people who reads the list of ingredients on food labels with growing dismay, you will be delighted to explore vegetarian alternatives. They are made, as far as possible, without preservatives, artificial colors or any other chemical additives. You can eat extremely well without compromising your health in any way.

Alfalfa: Alfalfa seeds contain incomplete protein. They are served as they are or as sprouts in salads and sandwiches. You can easily sprout alfalfa seeds yourself.

Arrowroot: A nutritive starch, used as a thickening agent, produced by the arrowroot or *maranta* plant.

Brewer's yeast: A food supplement that is rich in protein and vitamins from the B complex. A few spoonfuls can be added to baked goods for added nutrition. It is sold in its natural form and in a less bitter form as well.

Brown rice: Natural rice, not polished or refined in any way, with a crunchy texture.

Bulgur: Kernels of hard wheat that have been hulled and cooked. Bulgur is used as a cereal.

Carob: A crushed carob pod from a Mediterranean evergreen. Carob powder can be used in cooking as an alternative to chocolate.

Cottage cheese: A soft, bland white cheese made by allowing pasteurized milk to curdle and then draining off the buttermilk. It is highly nutritious but must be eaten within 48 hours of purchase because it quickly turns moldy, which ruins the taste.

Kasha: Grains of buckwheat, usually roasted and then boiled in water and served in the same way as rice.

Kefir: A fizzy, acid-tasting beverage made by fermenting buttermilk with yeast.

Millet: A type of cereal usually served in place of rice in main dishes. It is also sometimes served as a breakfast dish.

Miso: A paste made by mixing soybeans and salt with a cereal such as buckwheat, barley, rice or wheat. These ingredients are left to ferment for up to one year and then used to add flavor to soups, sauces and vegetables. Miso is very nutritious because it is rich in protein.

Sesame seeds:	These tiny seeds are rich in calcium and protein. They can be sprinkled on baked dishes (in place of breadcrumbs), on desserts or on the crusts of breads and buns.
Soybean:	The only type of bean that contains all the essential amino acids. It is a complete protein and can be readily used in place of meat.
Sunflower seeds:	Seeds with a distinctive black and white shell that are rich in minerals and protein. Sunflower seeds may be eaten alone as a snack or as part of cooked dishes.
Tamari:	A sauce made from soybeans and wheat.
Tempeh:	An Asian food prepared by fermenting soybeans with a type of mold that forms a white crust similar to that on Camembert cheese. It can be seasoned, toasted or roasted like meat.
Tofu:	A cheese-like substance made from soy milk. It is an excellent source of protein but has a rather bland taste, so tofu dishes are best made with aromatics or condiments that will add flavor.
Vegetable pâté:	Vegetable pâté is a classic vegetarian dish and is made from soybeans and spices. It is an excellent alternative to the more usual meat and liver pâtés.
Wheat germ:	The embryo of the wheat kernel, wheat germ contains a large quantity of Vitamin E. Uncooked wheat germ must be kept cool to preserve its vitamin content.

Conversion Chart

Conversion Chart for the Main Measures Used in Cooking

Volume
1 teaspoon........... 5 mL
1 tablespoon........ 15 mL

1 quart (4 cups)....... 1 litre
1 pint (2 cups)....... 500 mL
1/2 cup........... 125 mL
1/4 cup........... 50 mL

Weight
2.2 lb.......... 1 kg (1000 g)
1.1 lb............... 500 g
0.5 lb............... 225 g
0.25 lb.............. 115 g

1 oz................. 30 g

Metric Equivalents for Cooking Temperatures

49°C	120°F	120°C	250°F
54°C	130°F	135°C	275°F
60°C	140°F	150°C	300°F
66°C	150°F	160°C	325°F
71°C	160°F	180°C	350°F
77°C	170°F	190°C	375°F
82°C	180°F	200°C	400°F
93°C	200°F	220°C	425°F
107°C	225°F	230°C	450°F

Readers will note that, in the recipes, we give 250 mL as the equivalent for 1 cup and 450 g as the equivalent for 1 lb and that fractions of these measurements are even less mathematically accurate. The reason for this is that mathematically accurate conversions are just not practical in cooking. Your kitchen scales are simply not accurate enough to weigh 454 g—the true equivalent of 1 lb—and it would be a waste of time to try. The conversions given in this series, therefore, necessarily represent approximate equivalents, but they will still give excellent results in the kitchen. No problems should be encountered if you adhere to either metric or imperial measurements throughout a recipe.

Index

MICROTIPS